Race Issues ON THE WORLD SCENE

Dedicated to my wife, **Molly Conant**

Contents

Introduction

Most of the nations of the world are engaged in an unprecedented effort to improve the welfare of their peoples; much effort and money is being expended on research and surveys, on technical equipment and construction. Throughout the world men are being trained to bring techniques developed in one center to another; educational facilities are expanding, means of communication are improving, power is being made available, and health problems are being attacked. Natural, technological, and human resources are being mobilized increasingly for a widespread attack upon poverty.

Yet, for a variety of reasons, there are many areas of the world in which groups of peoples are unable to play fully effective roles in their societies. They may be excluded from certain occupations, living areas, and institutions; they may be restricted in their legal rights, they may be denied a political voice, and they may find the avenues to education and social advance closed to them. The reasons for their exclusion may be based on color, physical characteristics, different cultural and religious backgrounds, and the fact of colonial rule; or the reasons may be lost in antiquity. Although the reasons for their exclusion may be complex, the result is clear: any society which contains groups of people which are not regarded as contributing or able to contribute to the advance of the society as a whole, or which contains groups politically and socially isolated, is a society seriously crippled in its effort to progress. Coupled with this practical consideration is the growing view that discrimination violates the concept of the dignity and equality of men.

Belief in the value of man as an individual has produced a vigorous social and political revolution whose effects have been felt in

ix

the New World, in many areas of Africa, the Near East, and Asia. It is a belief which has gained extraordinary strength in a relatively short period of time; it has deep significance to all peoples in our world of today. Perhaps the most provocative charge today within the United Nations is that one group or nation contains or is ruling groups not considered or treated as equals.

In our concern with human welfare too much emphasis has been placed upon technological or economic advance. Problems of relations among men cannot be resolved in nuclear laboratories or by chemical formulae; the barriers between men are conceived in the minds of men. These barriers may be overthrown in time by a process of rapid and comprehensive economic and political change, but in the meantime they seriously impede the forces for change and development. Long after the barriers have disappeared, however, discrimination and personal indignities will persist and be important.

Scholars, politicians, statesmen, policemen, social workers, and administrators are involved in the problems posed by differences believed to exist between peoples. Some study the problems primarily to enlarge the knowledge of mankind, others to exploit the differences; still others study the problems to control them or to be able to advocate policies to reduce frictions within societies and between nations. Hawaii is an outstanding example of a locality in which studies for all of the above reasons have been made at one time or another.

The interracial character of Hawaii has been a fundamental feature of its modern history. Peoples from Japan, Korea, Okinawa, China, the Philippines, Europe, the Caribbean, and the mainland United States have dissolved a significant part of their differences in their common interest in rapid and extensive economic, social, and political growth. In this setting, the scholars of the University of Hawaii have had a unique opportunity to analyze the inhibiting power of race differences and the accelerating effect their gradual removal has on the advance of society as a whole.

The setting of Hawaii in the mid-Pacific has given its experience in race relations a unique importance in the twentieth century. Community leaders and scholars of the University appreciated early the value of their experience to many areas vitally concerned with the problems of minority and race relationships. Shortly after World War II, an international conference on race relations was proposed by the Department of Sociology of the University of Hawaii, under the direction of Dr. Andrew W. Lind.

Such a conference was held in the summer of 1954, sponsored jointly by the University of Hawaii, the University of California (Berkeley), and the University of Chicago. Men came to the conference from many areas of the world and with diverse interests and experiences. All of them had played a part, in one way or another, in studies of race situations, and all were convinced of the basic importance of the nature of the relationships among men and the direct bearing those relationships have on the welfare and advance of society. They met to exchange information on the problems and areas with which they were familiar. There was no intention on the part of the conference officers or on the part of the overwhelming majority of its members that the conference would result in a manifesto or declaration of views on race or race situations.

The objectives of the conference were limited: a setting would be created in which firsthand information would be made available and discussed, differences in analysis would be explained, and administrative policies for dealing with race situations would be compared. These discussions were not held in a vacuum; with a rich and varied background of direct experience, conference members were fully conscious of describing situations in which human beings were involved—often tragically.

Conference membership included sociologists, anthropologists, historians, economists, administrators, political scientists, and journalists. All were experienced in race situations in the United States, Central and South America, the Caribbean, Europe, the Union of Soviet Socialist Republics, Africa, the Near East, Southern

Asia, and the Pacific area. While a comprehensive review of all major race problems would have been impossible and was not attempted, a number of issues were given a world-wide perspective; they were examined in their immediate settings but not in those terms alone, for the purpose of the conference was to examine them in relation to the world significance of the human problems they represented.

From the outset, little limit was placed on the definition of "race." No narrow concept of "race" would meet the problem of analyzing the complex phenomena presented in race situations. For one conference member, one discipline might provide him with a methodology enabling him to gain insight into his interest; for another member, a different academic approach would prove more useful. On the other hand, an administrator, or a political observer, or a journalist would be less interested in methodology than in the understanding an analysis would provide him of a particular, practical problem. There was a broad hospitality to all methodologies; in the opinion of a number of the conference members, for example, a historian of the Near East provided some of the most provocative thinking on race problems in world perspective. In the opinion of the author, with his interest in Asian political affairs, the lasting value of the conference came, not from the focus of any particular discipline, but from the fact that issues of race were examined critically and in a world setting in which their political importance was evident. Their significance was accepted by all participants, and an effort was made to describe the effects that *industrialization, urbanization, improved communications,* and *political consciousness* have had on a number of race situations in many areas. In these descriptions, no one discipline monopolized.

Conference discussions of specific race situations demonstrated their complex and varied origins. In their development, they have passed through different stages and have been influenced by a host of factors. Race issues in the New World, in Europe, Africa, and the Soviet Union, in Southern Asia and the Pacific appear to have only one common denominator: the fact that human beings are involved. Religious differences, historical experiences, physical differences, language, economic factors, political issues and ideologies, social and cultural factors, migrations, international pressures, nationalism, labor requirements, urbanization, education, and communications are only a few of the many factors creating, heightening, or lessening racial tensions.

This book, written by a layman member of the conference, is a personal summary of many of the discussions and parts of conference papers. It reviews a number of race situations in the light of economic, political, and ideological forces in our contemporary world: among the American and African Negroes, among the Chinese in Southeast Asia, among the people of the Near East, Soviet Central Asia, the South Pacific, and Hawaii. The Conference Committee hopes that this review will stimulate interest in contemporary race issues in many parts of the world.

Rather than have a large number of footnotes scattered throughout the book, I have listed at the beginning of each chapter those papers from which ideas and quotations were taken. (In a few instances quotations have been taken from an early draft of a paper and do not appear in the paper as it was revised for publication.) Those interested in the complete papers are referred to the conference collection edited by Dr. Lind.*

Conference members have already recorded their great appreciation to Dr. Lind for his primary role in convening the conference. I would like to take this opportunity to express again my thanks to him and to the other members of the original conference committee: Dr. Herbert Blumer and Dr. Everett Hughes; and to their respective sponsoring institutions: the University of Hawaii, the University of California, and the University of Chicago. Assistance from the Ford Foundation and from the McInerny Foundation of Hawaii made it possible for the conference to be an international one.

* Andrew W. Lind, ed., *Race Relations in World Perspective* (Honolulu: University of Hawaii Press, 1955).

Mrs. Clarence Glick, conference recorder, did a very competent job in summarizing daily discussions. The excellence of her reports made this book possible. My wife and Dr. and Mrs. Neal Bowers provided editorial assistance and I am grateful to them. Mr. and Mrs. Howard Bryan gave generously of their time in typing the many drafts.

MELVIN CONANT

Honolulu, Hawaii
September, 1955

Race Issues ON THE WORLD SCENE

Chapter 1

RACE IN THE CONTEMPORARY WORLD

Sources utilized in this chapter include, in addition to the conference reports and discussions, the following papers in Andrew W. Lind, ed., Race Relations in World Perspective *(Honolulu: University of Hawaii Press, 1955), "Reflections on Theory of Race Relations," by Herbert G. Blumer; "Rigidity and Fluidity in Race Relations," by Bernhard L. Hormann; and "Occupation and Race on Certain Frontiers," by Andrew W. Lind.*

The Meaning of Race

At the outset of the conference, attention was drawn to the fact that "race" means many different things, depending upon one's training and experience and purpose. The narrow concept of race as a biological term, however useful it may be in attempting to classify "types" of human beings, is of little value in terms of studies of "race relations." Here we are concerned far more with the complex social and cultural problems which arise from contact between people who consider themselves, or are considered by others, to be different. "Races, from this point of view, exist when groups identify each other as such, however ludicrous these identifications may be from the point of view of the biological scientist."

Perhaps the closest the conference came to considering a "definition" of race was in the Commission on Race Relations in World Perspective, set up within the conference as a special study group. A number of conference members participated actively in its work. This commission reported a statement which reflected the approach of a majority of the participants:

3

In all societies there are tensions and conflicts between groups. In many societies men are conscious of real or fictitious differences of "race" between groups—differences of color, of origin, and so on. "Racial problems" arise when ideas of racial difference become interwoven with the struggles of groups. Groups may struggle for power, or land, or economic advantage, or because of differing conceptions of the truth; ideas of race may be involved in the conflicts as symbols of deeper differences, but they may also themselves be important causes of conflict.[1]

While this view was a common thread which ran through most discussions, it was by no means universally accepted. In fact, it was the subject of a vigorous dissent by a European and by an Asian, neither of whom found it possible to examine race relations—as the former expressed it—in terms so "vague, wide, and, in respect of color, inaccurate." To him, the conference should have concerned itself with the *facts* of race and not the *ideas* of race. The Asian member, significantly, sought eagerly for a formal conference resolution denying the validity of the view that "race" and "culture" or levels of achievement had any necessary connection. His concern on this point was not shared by either the African members present or the overwhelming number of conference delegates who were reluctant at a scholarly convention to decide any issue by vote. In fact, the majority were surprised that this particular issue, no longer considered relevant in most scientific circles, should have been raised at all.

However, the intensity of this discussion reflected the dramatic problem of race in the contemporary world. Race is not a subject for scholarly inquiry alone; it is a political issue of extraordinary vitality. There is scarcely a region which does not contain in some degree an element of a race problem. In many areas it has an explosive force unequalled by any other issue. While the concern of many is focused today on race as an issue expressed most frequently in terms of black or brown versus white, this polarization of the

---

[1] The Commission on Race Relations in World Perspective, "Race Relations: The World Perspective" (mimeographed; in the files of the Sociology Department, University of Hawaii, Honolulu, Hawaii).

problem is unfortunate and misleading. It excludes often a sober consideration of race problems within Asia, for example, which cannot be described so neatly. This polarization tends also to exclude other aspects of race in which color difference is not the factor used to distinguish groups of people as races.

The concern of the Asian conference member was understandable, in terms of the historical and political experience through which his people have passed—an experience in which his fellow men heard that the justification of foreign control lay in their declared inability or unfitness to rule, often because of their alleged inferiority to European man. However, several conference members suggested that this experience did not apply to European man alone; that within Asia, throughout history, there have been concepts of "superiority" found in the history of Chinese relations and, before World War II, in the slogans of Japanese expansionists. More recently, the tragic communal riots in India and Pakistan may be said to have included race issues, broadly defined. These instances were not advanced to minimize in any way the contribution that European man had made to race situations but did serve to give wider perspective to the discussion.

All of these factors were kept in mind by the members of the conference; in fact, it would have been impossible to have attracted to the meeting men of such diverse interests if issues in race relations were to be discussed as phenomena isolated from the contemporary world. All present were conscious that a major reason for holding the conference stemmed from the fact that hundreds of millions of people have become aware of race, and the subject is of profound importance to all.

The Study of Race

Initial conference sessions were concerned necessarily with suggestions of various methods of analysis. Here again the emphasis lay on the dynamic aspect of race situations. An American member began by asking the conference to consider this dynamic quality and to recognize that sociological phenomena are involved in race situations; men are not biological specimens alone. Problems in race relations arise not through occasional or infrequent contact but through prolonged association. Eventually, this association between groups considered to be races results in a *system* of relationships, and a complex set of operating factors becomes involved which regularizes the positions of the groups. For example, a dominant group may reserve to itself certain political positions, occupations, and social levels. Thus, in parts of the United States, notably the South, the Negro traditionally has his "place." This reservation of status and role exists in the current racial policies of the Union of South Africa. (The most striking and perhaps oldest example occurs in the caste system of India, the origins of which are still obscure.) In other parts of Africa and in South Asia, numerous examples of reserved occupations may be found, although these are undergoing rapid change.

Where there are status and role differentiations there will be "social distance"—i.e., reserved roles isolating one group from another. An American conference member suggested that from studies of status, role, and social distance one can explore race problems in terms of prejudice, exploitation, and change. A British member with experience in Africa questioned if one could even make an analysis of race relations as such; in fact, the attempt to isolate race factors in such terms might obscure rather than clarify a race situation. There are many pressures bearing on group relations; there is a much larger "web of relationships" in which considerations of race, even very broadly defined, may prove to be only a few strands.

For example, one could not ignore the different historical experiences of Africans in Central Africa and West Africa—experiences which may be responsible in part for the difference in race relations in these two areas. The kinds of economic relationships which developed in Central Africa and in British West Africa were offered as a case in point. In Central Africa, as a whole, a definite color bar exists. In British West Africa (especially Nigeria and the Gold Coast),

Africans participate significantly in the legislature, and no official color bar is upheld. The fact that there are permanent European settlers in Central Africa and not in West Africa has been one reason offered in the past to explain this difference in attitude in areas which have been under British control for many years. But the reason lies deeper and in a still larger context. In West Africa, the British are committed to a policy of growing African participation in the life of their land, but in Central Africa strong pressure opposes any change in existing relationships. In economic activity, West Africans produce materials for export and constitute an important market for imports. British firms here would oppose any "reactionary" trend in racial policy or attitude. In Central Africa, on the other hand, the need for African labor and the close association between British firms in England and those in Africa leads to opposition in Parliament to views which would alter existing relationships and which would bring greater African participation. These several examples of the larger setting in which race relationships occur were offered as evidence of the need for studying these problems in their settings. Thus, a study of the status and role of the American Negro which did not consider the fundamental effect of changing economic conditions would be incomplete.

The matter of fluidity or change in race situations should be examined in the light of a number of forces of modern society which have their impact on race problems. An American who had extensive experience in race problems in labor relations suggested that some of these forces stem from the marked and continuous change in technology. These changes affect human relationships in developed areas and are having a fundamental effect in undeveloped regions. The availability of industrial power will alter markedly the whole pattern of relationships in parts of Africa, the Middle East, and Asia, just as it has already had a pervasive influence in the southern parts of the United States. Another force in modern society is urbanization, closely linked with the application of technology to, or the more effective exploitation of, hitherto unused resources. Growing demands for labor have a magnetic influence and draw into areas people who leave behind them their communities with traditional social controls and customs.

Still another basic operating force is communication. The rapid spread of ideas into areas which were relatively isolated a decade ago has inevitably brought new information and new ideas to many millions of people. Not all of these ideas are concerned with technology; they have alerted many to new political and social beliefs and to new concepts and standards of equality, opportunity, and conduct which have deeply disturbed existing relationships. In addition, there is the important factor of increased organization of people into interest and pressure groups along occupational, political, recreational, community, and other lines. These organizations may reflect established interests or serve to forward new ones; they may seek to preserve the status quo or initiate change. All of these factors have had an important influence on the changing character of race situations and must be considered in any analysis.

There were several other approaches discussed at the conference and one of these was the concept of the "frontier"—the zone of transition, so to speak, in which peoples meet and where new peoples and cultures develop. This zone of transition may be both an area of tension and accommodation, for in it one finds struggles between groups within the frontier—or zone of contact—and also, in some cases, with groups outside the immediate area when the conflict involves a colonial people and their rulers. These frontiers may be "race-creating" as well as "race-destroying" situations. They embrace all aspects of the society involved and provide a useful area of analysis.

Race Frontiers

The concept of the frontier was implicit in many of the reports before the conference. The trading frontier, cultural frontier, political frontier, and missionary frontier are all found in race situations in Africa, the Middle East, Southeast Asia, and in the

New World. A leading conference member offered a special analysis of the problems of occupation and race in the plantation frontier, mining frontier, farm settlement frontier, and commercial frontier. Implicit in this analysis is the critical influence of economic conditions on patterns of race relationships. This critical economic factor may stem from a variety of circumstances, but it usually expresses itself in occupational differentiation on a racial basis; it is important to note, however, that this economic reference does not exclude other factors and that what may begin in an economic setting eventually may include political and cultural factors as well; what begins as a struggle for existence becomes in many instances a struggle for status or freedom. Appreciation of the changing character of race relations forces one to discard, as an oversimplification, any notion that race is a "phenomenon of the capitalist exploitation of peoples and its complementary attitudes,"[2] or that racial prejudice is the "expression of the effort of white ruling groups to preserve their position."

If one uses the frontier as the area to be studied, one must recognize two possible results of new economic activity. One effect is the "freeing" of societies as the use of technology increases and new skills are acquired. Another effect is that in some areas opportunities for economic expansion may conflict with established interests which, if they represent the dominant political group, may lead to more rigid occupational divisions and further restrictions in political activities.

Futhermore, there can be no particular forecast of the kind of race situations which will evolve from a frontier situation, for each has its special conditions leading to particular problems. To illustrate this, the conference was asked to consider three types of economic frontiers—the plantation frontier, the settlement frontier, and the commercial frontier.

[2] Quoted from Oliver Cromwell Cox in Andrew W. Lind, ed., *Race Relations in World Perspective* (Honolulu: University of Hawaii Press, 1955), "Occupations and Race on Certain Frontiers," by Andrew W. Lind.

The plantation is, as one member described it, a "race-making" situation. It is so because of the distinctive problems of adequate labor supply. Plantations tend to develop in areas of relatively sparse population or in areas where the available labor supply is, for one reason or another, unwilling or unable to work under a regulated system. The plantation system calls for controlled labor and in many areas this has resulted in the importation of laborers. The managerial level of the plantation is usually of a different race from the indigenous or imported peoples and it is from this fact that the plantation becomes a "race-making" situation. This is particularly true since the conditions for plantation employment commonly involve a degree of servitude. Various forms of contract labor bring the worker to the plantation theoretically for the duration of an agreement but usually for a longer period. The obvious differences in standards of living, areas of residence, and privileges of the managerial group and the laborers emphasize other differences and tend to complicate the element of race, and to increase tensions between the two groups. Problems arise also between imported laborers and the indigenous peoples. There is also a functional character of race when it is used by plantations to define and preserve the status and functions of groups working within the plantation system. The race-making aspects of the system rest, then, in distinctions in the status and role of the laborers who are usually racially different from management. These circumstances give rise to a hierarchic system of racial emphases within the plantation system which mark clearly the basic difference between the plantation frontier and the frontier of settlement.

Race appears to enter into the settlement frontier because of the special character, extent, and competitive implications of land ownership. In the settlement frontier, the avid interest in the land on the part of the small, aggressive, relatively powerful, and better organized immigrant minority, usually of a racial background different from that of the indigenous peoples whose properties are sought, is bound to result in a conflict of some intensity between the two groups.

When one group of people moves into a new area, the question of labor may be unimportant and this element of racial tension does not arise. The control of the better land is the focus of the conflict. In areas such as Kenya, where the better land is monopolized by a few who are racially distinct from the indigenous peoples, the race issue becomes symbolic of the clash of interests and, as in the plantation frontier, the race symbol quickly comes to represent a host of factors reflective of differentiating characteristics such as customs, religion, and fact of political power. In time, and if the activity of the dominant minority results in an expanding economic system, there may develop new contacts between the groups, with the indigenous peoples acquiring new interests which may be supplementary to those of the dominant group.

The commercial frontier is different from either the plantation or the settlement. In the commercial area there are not the marked racial and community divisions characteristic of the other frontiers. The development of trading and industrial centers attracts peoples from rural areas. Initially they may form new groups among themselves on a racial basis, as is happening in Africa, with economic development programs and urbanization. But the atmosphere of the market tends to resolve such differences with greater contacts between racial groups, at least in the economic world. From contacts between racial groups may arise social relations and, eventually, political associations which dissolve or lessen the importance of the original racial barriers.

The usefulness of the "frontier" approach was of interest to many. At the same time it was recognized that none of the race situations typified one kind of frontier or another. The commercial frontier develops frequently alongside plantation and settlement frontiers. From their interaction new areas of contact result in still more frontiers. The usefulness of the concept of the frontier is in its inclusiveness. It permits the observer to view race problems in terms of the economic, social, and cultural settings of the whole society.

Occupation and Race

One aspect of the economic frontier which should receive careful attention is the relationship between occupations and race. Reserved occupations are noted frequently in race situations. The examples of Malaya and Hawaii were offered. Both areas were involved in Western expansion in the nineteenth century; both developed extensive plantation systems, and each had a dominant trade outlet: Singapore in the case of Malaya, and Honolulu in the case of Hawaii. Yet, today there are basic differences between the two, differences which may be attributed in large part to the influence of the trading center on the outlying regions. Honolulu had an extensive influence on the plantation systems from the beginning. For many years, the number of people living in Honolulu has been much greater than the number living in rural areas—in contrast to the population of Singapore and Malaya. If one studies the occupational data of the two areas, one finds important evidence of the effect of the commercial frontier and the urban center on race. There is in Malaya a pronounced correlation between one's race and one's occupation; in Hawaii it is less obvious and is fast disappearing. The Europeans in Malaya have been chiefly the proprietors, managers, and senior staff of wholesale businesses, bank officials, military officers, and government administrators. The Malays are predominantly in small agriculture; few take part in government, the professions, or commerce. The Chinese are also engaged in agriculture and mining, but a significant proportion are in trade. In Hawaii, over the past quarter century, there has been a continuing spread of the members of various racial groups into a variety of occupations and a steady increase in the number reaching managerial, professional, and high government positions, both appointive and elective. Generally speaking, the oldest group of imported laborers —the Chinese—have risen highest in the economic scale, with Japanese, more recently arrived, following. Portuguese and Filipinos, most recent of all, rank relatively low. An American conference member suggested that occupational figures, considered in the setting of an economic frontier, might provide a useful tool of analysis for the study of trends in race situations.

Few aspects of race situations are as explosive as that of number. One of the constant arguments of the government of the Union of South Africa concerns the number of black Africans compared with people of European origin; the fear of being "swamped" is prominent in the justifications for the various racial policies of that government. But it is not only in South Africa that numbers are important. The issue arises in the United States, as well, when the racial character of urban areas changes. It is present also in the critical problem of the millions of overseas Chinese in Southeast Asia. The distrust between Hindus and Moslems, each fearing the influence of the other, led in part to the tragic decision to divide the Indian subcontinent.

Involved in these threats of numbers are basic conceptions of "struggles for existence" and "survival of the fittest"; there is an instinctive urge to preserve one's status and holdings. Complicating the issues which arise in such situations is widespread belief in universal suffrage, itself an expression of the equality—one man, one vote—which runs counter to many practices which either disenfranchise or restrict the extent of a group's participation in the national political and economic life.

Demography and Race

Studies of the demographic aspects of race relations may be of great value, since population trends have a significant bearing on race situations. Demographic research may help to throw light on relatively little-studied aspects of race problems: what happens, demographically, when one group comes in contact with another—especially when one group is markedly less "advanced" and its culture and organization seem inferior to the culture and organization of the other? A specific instance of such a study was reported by an Australian member whose primary interest was the response of the Australian aborigine to the coming of European man. Once

doomed to extinction, some aborigines have made partial adjustment and accommodated themselves to certain features of Australian
life. They are now increasing in numbers.

The contrasted demographic reactions of folk (nomadic or food-
gathering) and peasant peoples (settled agriculturists with some
trading experience) to contacts with other dominant peoples was
noted. In the case of folk peoples, the result has frequently been one
of initial decline, while in the case of peasant peoples there has been
an opposite response. However, there is an eventual reversal of this
trend, apparently, in the case of folk peoples, and certainly one of
the critical issues of today is whether peasant peoples will, after
their initial increase, respond to substantial economic change by a
stabilization of population.

Still another example of the importance of demographic research
was offered by an African who described the problem of Indians in
Africa. Africans seek to replace the Indian, who is usually more
skilled and frequently has another important economic role—that
of small merchant or middleman. The European in Africa is wary
of the Indian because of his business aptitudes and growing political
and racial consciousness. These African and European feelings are
expressed frequently in terms of the "numbers" of Indians. A
complicated race problem has emerged in which the concept of
numbers plays an important part and is used as a symbol of the
entire problem of Indians.

Changes in economic interests also have serious effects on race
relations. In Kenya, the ownership and use of the highlands is a
main issue, and the disparity in numbers between the Europeans
and Africans gives a special bitterness and sense of urgency to the
conflict. In Uganda, also, the increase in the number of permanent
European settlers with families is causing greater friction with
Africans. Demographic change with racial effects may result, in
other instances, from the search for economic opportunities. In
Southern Rhodesia and Portuguese East Africa it is interesting to
note that in this search Africans have drifted from areas where

race relations have been more harmonious to those where they are less so. Such a movement introduces Africans to different racial attitudes, and new or modified race problems occur.

Finally, several conference members indicated that the "perception of numbers" may be of greater symbolic importance in race studies than actual numbers would indicate. In Jamaica, the number of Chinese is small, but they are a conspicuous group owing to their role in trade. In Australia, the perception of the Chinese is not based on an actual head count of those living in Australia but of the hundreds of millions in China itself. Hence, in these cases strict demographic studies of race situations may on occasion lead to wrong analyses unless something more than actual numbers is considered.

Demographic studies may have special value in race situations if a study is made to shed light on the relationship between race situations and cultural or economic or political change; in this case, demography would depart, as a conference member expressed himself, from the traditional approach which deals with human populations "in the same terms as the population of fruit flies and equates population units without reference to culture." Here demographic studies of race relations would, in effect, abstract certain aspects of total race settings for examination. The demographic approach, like an economic study, provides clues but does not provide complete answers.

Stratification and Race

The critical influence of economic stratification on race relations was examined in terms of a number of specific situations and is reviewed in a later section. Consideration of economic stratification, while regarded by most of the conference members as being highly important, was not considered to be exclusively so or necessarily paramount. Economic conditions and economic change in relation to race relations emerged so frequently, however, that a

British member suggested that Karl Marx was an honorary ghost-member of the conference.

The influence of changing economic conditions has been marked on the American and African Negro, overseas Chinese, and others. Technological changes and changes in land use and industrialization have created new demands for labor and a greater need for skills and have altered values and standards of living. Occupations once reserved to certain groups are now being opened to others. The American Negro, for example, begins to achieve "white-collar" status. The African begins to move off the land and into urban areas. As a mine laborer or low-level civil servant he aspires to higher positions now open to him in some parts of Africa. Under the impact of economic change, the character of race relations is modified. Sometimes race tensions are lessened as a result of these changes and in other cases they are worsened. Sometimes the discriminated group loses its racial identity under new living and working conditions, and sometimes, as has happened with some Negroes, members of the racial group gain new conceptions of themselves.

In colonial areas of the world, the special economic role of the ruling group created and maintained an economic stratification which reflected the local race situation. The Dutch were initially the traders; the Javanese were the producers; the Chinese were the "handmaids of capitalism," occupying the middleman position. In Burma, India, and elsewhere, similar economic stratifications followed race lines. The colonial power had reserved functions. Nowhere is this aspect of race and economic status more evident than in the well-known case of the Anglo-Indian. His status as a distinct group in India was marked by occupations in the railways reserved deliberately for him by the British.

The relationship of social stratification to race situations was discussed with special reference to Brazil. According to an American, social stratification here has special value as an object of study because of the long tradition of miscegenation between the European,

Indian, and African peoples, the absence of violent racial conflicts, and the informal policy of the absorption of minorities into the "Brazilian population." (These attitudes stemmed in part from the historic association in Europe between Portuguese and Moors.) The result has been a division of Brazilian society, as one conference member expressed it, not in terms of race but in terms of one's status in society. Color plays a role in determining one's status but is only one of a number of determinants; family status, professional status, economic position, and education appear to be even more important.

A Unesco study of race relations in Brazil suggests that this picture does not apply to all areas; that in Rio de Janeiro, for example, an increase in race consciousness had been noted among various economic classes along with the influence of imported North American traditional views on Negroes. In some urban areas, this growing consciousness of race has been expressed in a "workers' party" and in the "Black Front"—an organization in the industrial areas based on color. A conference member pointed out that its motivation came from those who had suffered from economic competition with Italians. The further observation was made that "in the Amazon Valley a distinctive set of attitudes are held toward Indian ancestry. Here enslavement of the Indians continued into this century, and Indian ancestry is negatively valued because it signifies slave status in recent memory." The question was raised as to the practical value of a distinction being drawn between "race" and "color," with the implied denial of "racism" being involved when color was the basis of differentiation. Yet many consider a race situation to exist when one's color, facial structure, hair, eyes, or height is the basis of the distinction to which race symbols are attached whether that distinction is of primary importance or one of a number operating in the society. The importance of the Brazilian example lies more in the Brazilian emphasis on miscegenation and the assimilation of groups into the Brazilian population.

The concept of social stratification as a method of study was considered to be of value in studying Brazil and other areas of the New World. Race situations in Spanish America concern generally Indian-white relationships. Race situations vary from one nation to another, but, as a whole, Spanish America shares with Brazil the factor of social background or family being a major determinant in one's position, with considerations of color being only one element.

In Mexico in the eighteenth and nineteenth centuries, a racial colonial society was established with an elite white group at the top, mestizos in the middle, and Indians at the base. Today, with the disappearance of the white elite as the dominant group, mestizos have emerged as the ruling group, and race is no longer an important factor in social stratification. There is infinite gradation of racial type and of status which precludes any rigid classification. Today, the term "Indian" indicates more a way of life out of which one can pass, thereby losing the "Indian" identity. Brazil and Mexico are instances, therefore, where analyses of social stratification contribute to an understanding of the influence of race, and this may be true for any area where miscegenation has occurred on a wide scale. *interbreeding*

In other areas of South America, such as Peru and Bolivia, race issues have arisen. In the former, the plantation system continues to impose a rigid social system; the number of Indians who have moved into the towns is regarded with some anxiety. The Indian is regarded as inferior and as a danger to society. In Bolivia, on the other hand, the element of race has been introduced along with the economic changes which have occurred and has resulted in a glorification of Indian blood. One member remarked on the growth of Indian race consciousness since World War I. The influence of Communists in this development was noted by another member who described the various steps taken by the Comintern and other groups to encourage it.

The closing sessions of the conference on various approaches to the study of race relations considered the usefulness of racial stratification as a conceptual scheme. Two conference members with long

African experience agreed this approach would help bring out elements of race situations but thought it would not be the key to full understanding of complex problems. Racial stratification implies the existence of a body of customs and doctrine legitimizing a hierarchical system based on a racial division of the people. Position and roles are defined. At first glance, South and East Africa seem useful examples where this situation applies. There is race stratification, with Europeans at the top, Indians and others in between, and Africans at the bottom. Certain economic roles are performed by each group. There is general acceptance of a political control. However, conflicting backgrounds and interests have produced deep divisions within each stratification. Some Africans are beginning to form an elite group. Dynamic forces are present and growing: industrialization, urbanization, new ideologies, and loyalties. These parts of Africa cannot conform to the suggested conceptual scheme, for here, as in so many other places, the emphasis must be placed on the dynamics of the situation rather than on a search for static characteristics. Methods developed for the study of race relations in modern societies of the West may be inappropriate and even misleading when applied to Africa, the Middle East, and Asia. In many areas tribal identifications and blood relationships determine social and political groupings without the concept of race. When new elements, such as European domination and control or Indian merchants, appear on the scene, and each group is obviously identifiable by color, then color becomes identified with position, and a problem of race—using a broad definition—arises.

The Total Study of Race

The injection into conference discussion of various methods for analyzing race situations raised the question as to whether race relations may be theoretically abstracted for useful study from their total setting in society. It was held by several that this could and should be done. A view more generally held was that race relations can be most effectively studied as an integral part of the whole society. The great majority of the conference papers used this "total" approach and this view dominated the conference.

An Asian suggested that of all the factors that might be abstracted the political factor and its influence on race relations was dominant. To him, the formula which exerts the greatest influence in race situations is "white men may rule whites; whites may rule non-whites; nonwhites may rule nonwhites but nonwhites may not rule whites." He asked if concern about race did not reflect the worry of whites about their loss of power over nonwhites. Was not this essentially an expression of their concern over future relationships with nonwhites? This provocative remark led to a discussion of the more important forces in today's race situations.

Western Man and Race

The most important commission of the conference, the Commission on Race Relations in World Perspective, dealt largely with ideas of race and their historical settings. In the commission's report, race was considered "as an *idée force,* an element in a historical process," and the report was concerned more with the extent of its influence than with the limits of its scientific validity. The report described how, during the last four hundred years, the intellectual and technical revolution which took place in Europe spread gradually to a large part of the world. In the process a few Western nations established their own domination over a great part of that world.

This domination took many forms: indirect control by economic and other means, political control without European settlement, political control leading to European settlement, and the creation in the New World of multiracial states with groups of European origin dominant over other groups of immigrants or emancipated slaves. The establishment and maintenance of control led inevitably to a certain separation between the dominant group and others, both because of the necessities of power and because of differences in culture and standards of life.

As a subsidiary element in this process, there gradually arose various ideas of "white superiority." They were molded, on the one hand, by the facts that "white" peoples had power, and that they could not have had power had they not possessed certain sorts of superiority—in technical mastery and the arts of domination; on the other, by the context of ideas in which they emerged—by such ideas as those of "Christendom," "civilizing mission," "progress," and the "survival of the fittest." As they emerged, these racial ideas came to play an important role in the systems of "white" domination. They served to explain and justify that domination to the "white" peoples themselves and to their subjects; they helped not only to justify but to make more rigid the system of separation which followed almost necessarily from the fact of power. In so doing they helped to create, among both rulers and ruled, certain ways of thinking and acting which need more detailed study than they have yet received.

The first effect of Western expansion was to shake the existing social and economic systems in Asia, Africa, and the Americas, and to weaken the power of resistance among their peoples. Many of them acquiesced in European power for a time, but not forever. As the new forces released by European rule reshaped their economic and social life, they became ever more unwilling to accept the position of inferiority to which the Western organization of the world consigned them; and the idea of "white superiority," with all its effects on the behavior of individuals and groups, offended their sense of human dignity. Thus there took place a re-creation of group-consciousness among the subjected peoples, which expressed itself largely in forms adopted from Europe and America. Over against the racial ideas of the "white peoples" there developed in some regions a sense of racial solidarity and self-assertion among the "nonwhites." But the movement of revolt adopted other ideas as well. For the idea of racial superiority never gathered to itself the totality of beliefs and attitudes which make up Western civilization. In fact, it was in direct contradiction with such doctrines as those of equality, liberty, and the rule of law, which the West has derived from its Greek, Roman, and Christian heritage, and which have deeply influenced the ways of life and thought of the Western peoples. Europe sent out its ideas as well as its goods and its armies; simply by belonging to a world dominated by the West, the subject peoples eventually became aware of its basic principles. Thus their movements of revolt drew power from ideas which the Western world itself recognized as valid; at the same time, they looked for inspiration to their own inherited cultures, in some of which (in those of Islam and Hinduism, for example) similar doctrines were embedded.

These movements of revolt, both by their very existence and by the forms in which they were expressed, reacted in their turn upon the mind, imagination, and conscience of Western man....

The age of European supremacy is passing. Two world wars and further developments in the technical revolution have changed the distribution of power in the world; and a heightened awareness of the contradiction between the moral and political principles which have created Western society and the facts of the old colonial system has helped to bring about a change in conceptions and methods of rule. The Western Powers are withdrawing, willingly or otherwise, from countries which they previously governed. In other countries the nature of the control they still retain is being modified; for example, the Commonwealth is taking shape as the British Empire disappears. In the United States also the pattern of race relations established after the emancipation of the slaves is being transformed by the accelerated working out, under the rule of law, of the ideas of liberty and equality. This process of withdrawal and change is gradually modifying the social system established by European power and the ideas elaborated to justify it. But here the change comes more slowly; there is a time lag between the shift in the distribution of power and the consequent changes in the ideas and behavior. Some of the problems of the present moment arise from this time lag. In the world as a whole, ideas of racial equality are emerging over against the racial ideologies of the past century; and some thinkers are questioning the validity of the biological idea of "race" when applied to human society and culture. This process is affected by the rise of world Communism, which has substituted "class" for "race" as the basic category for the understanding of multiracial societies. In some places, however, racial ideas are being strengthened rather than weakened. As European power ebbs it leaves behind it, in different parts of Africa, "islands" of settlers, some of them long established in their regions of settlement, who cling to their ideas of difference and habits of separation. Among the once subject peoples, resentment against their former rulers still tends to take a "racial" color. Moreover, since the end of European dominance new tensions have emerged between and within the newly independent states, and these too may be colored by racial ideas, the legacies of Western rule, or of some still earlier historical experience.

The changes in power, and the resultant changes in ideas and feelings and behavior, create complex problems of adjustment.[3]

Examples of these changes and adjustments are found in practically all race situations. In this context, American and African Negroes were discussed, followed by reports on race situations in the Pacific and Asia.

---

[3] The Commission on Race Relations in World Perspective, *op. cit.*

Chapter 2

THE AMERICAN AND THE AFRICAN NEGRO

Sources utilized in this chapter include, in addition to the conference reports and discussions, the following papers in Andrew W. Lind, ed., Race Relations in World Perspective *(Honolulu: University of Hawaii Press, 1955), "The Negro in the United States," by E. Franklin Frazier; "Race Relations in the Development of Southern Africa," by John A. Barnes; and "Race Relations in South Africa," by Absolum Vilakazi.*

The American Negro

From a Racial Problem to a Racial Minority. The changes taking place in the position of the American Negro were among the more dramatic examples of the fluidity in race situations today discussed at the race relations conference. As a leading Negro scholar described the present situation in the United States, the American Negro is now mentioned less in terms of a *racial problem* and more in terms of a *racial minority.* Changes in his position have resulted from the rapid social, political, and economic progress made in the United States in the last several generations.

Studies of the American Negro must be based, the conference was told, on a fundamental appreciation of the economic and political developments which have occurred in our time. From such studies emerge two important conclusions: changes in the social, political, and economic status of the Negro have occurred because of the increased demand for labor in industrial centers. Coupled with these were basic changes in rural economic life which, in turn, resulted in an extensive shift in the location of Negroes in many areas of the country. Thus, the American Negro, as discussed in the conference,

23

is a useful example of the effect economic circumstances may have on race problems. The American Negro is also an important example of two of the other conference themes: the influence of urbanization on race relations and the undoubted effect changes in public attitudes have on the status of racial minorities.   p. 21

Negroes are believed to have been brought first to what is now the United States in 1619. Their rate of increase was very slow until the eighteenth century, when the first of a number of basic changes in the American economy occurred with the introduction of commercial agriculture. This enterprise had an important effect upon the Negro, especially in the South. At the end of the eighteenth century, one out of every five inhabitants of the United States was a Negro, and 40 per cent of them lived in Virginia alone. The North contained only some 10 per cent of the Negroes, largely in the Middle Atlantic coastal states. As an indication of the labor demands of commercial agriculture, the number of slave Negroes increased from 700,000 to almost 4,000,000 in the period 1790 to 1860.

The Economic Role of the American Negro. Originally, economic considerations were important in relegating the Negro to slave status; racial considerations as such were probably not of major importance. The status of Negro servants became differentiated from that of white servants for labor reasons, "adaptability" to plantation life, and the greater control which could be exercised over them. The continued and growing importance of plantation agriculture facilitated the growth of Negro slavery in the South, while in the North, early in the nineteenth century, different and changing economic patterns virtually ended slavery.

With this economic advantage, efforts were made by Southerners to justify slavery on moral and religious grounds. According to a Negro conference member, two of the first sociology books published in America offered a philosophical justification of slavery.

Yet, in certain areas of the South, an increasing number of Negroes found themselves free for a variety of reasons. Some bought their freedom, others were given it as a reward for service, and a large

number were released as changing economic conditions altered traditional patterns, notably in Virginia and North Carolina, where free
Negroes became owners of small farms. Those who went to the cities
were generally better off than the northern urban Negroes; there was
relatively little competition in southern cities from European immigrants and opportunities were open for Negroes to become artisans.
The southern Negro faced competition from poor whites only after
emancipation had, in effect, freed both groups from the control of
large land- and slave-owning whites.

In the latter part of the nineteenth century, most Negroes lived
in the "Black Belt" of the South Atlantic states. During this period a
large number of Negroes left the rural areas for the urban centers
of the South, and a small number migrated to the North. Despite this
trend, commercial agriculture remained supreme, and, by the end of
the nineteenth century, some 80 per cent of the Negroes were still
living in southern rural areas.

The pattern in the North, where the economic system was
markedly different, was sharply reversed. Whereas the greater majority of Negroes in the South were in the countryside, practically
all the northern Negroes were in cities. Concurrent with the growth
of industrial labor opportunities, the historic drift has been increasingly from the rural areas to the cities, in the South as well as in the
North. The "Black Belt" has continued to lose its Negro population
to the North with mass migrations to New York, Chicago, Detroit,
and Philadelphia. This movement has overshadowed the southern
urbanization drift; in fact, the extent of the migrations to northern
cities was and is of critical importance to the steady change in the
position of the American Negro. In the past ten years alone there
has been a Negro population movement of great size—comparable
perhaps only to the nineteenth-century flow of immigrants to the
United States. Two million Negroes left the South between 1940
and 1950, and the migration continues. There has not been one
metropolitan region of the United States in which the increase of
the nonwhite population has not been in the neighborhood of at

least 50 per cent. Two world wars accelerated this trend until today the percentage of Negroes in United States cities has risen from 23 per cent in 1900 to 63 per cent in 1950. This transformation of the picture of the location of American Negroes is a direct result of striking changes in the American economy: the decreased importance of labor in the cash crops and the demand for industrial workers.

By 1914, 90 per cent of the Negroes were still in the South, but evidence of important economic change lay in the fact that one-fourth of the Negro farmers were farm owners; three-fourths were tenants. There was evidence that the position of the southern Negro at least was in the process of being stabilized. From 1910 to 1950 the most dramatic change of all occurred with the introduction of Negroes, in increasing numbers, into the extensive growth of the American industrial economy. The per cent of unskilled Negro male labor dropped from 63.3 per cent to 35 per cent; that of female unskilled labor from 88.4 per cent to 50.3 per cent. Unskilled male farm labor dropped from 30 per cent to 10 per cent, while the percentage of semiskilled male Negroes rose from 3.6 per cent in 1910 to 34.4 per cent in 1950. Negro female semiskilled labor rose from 5.4 per cent in 1910 to 33.6 per cent in 1950. The most significant shift was away from the soil. In the period from 1910 to 1950, the number of Negro male farm owners, tenants, and unskilled farm laborers declined from 56.1 per cent of the employed Negro force to 23.3 per cent.

The proportion of Negro male skilled workers in the North today is nearly twice as great as in the South. Of special importance is the far larger number of male and female Negroes in clerical and sales positions. In the North there are nearly four times as many, and in the West, whose Negro population has risen greatly in recent decades, there are at least three times as many in these jobs as in the South.

A number of reasons account for the sectional differences in the position of the American Negro, and all are important in the study of race relations. First, there is the *relative* absence of race barriers to occupations in the North as compared with the South. Second, the Negro vote has become an important factor, and the Negro has, accordingly, found a place in white-collar occupations in municipal government. Third, in more recent years, a number of court decisions and legislative acts affecting Negroes and Negro rights have had a great effect on their position in the American community. Coupled with these acts and decisions has been a heightened interest in their status by people in social welfare, public administration, and private groups concerned with minorities and race relations in the United States. Labor unions have also played a significant part, as have the armed forces. These factors have produced an important change in the Negro status in the North and West; they have had little impact, comparatively speaking, in the South as reported by a Negro conference member.

The low economic position of Negroes in American life is still important, however, when one considers the relative proportion of skilled Negro workers to the total number of Negroes employed: one out of every thirteen employed Negro men is in a skilled occupation—contrast this with the figure that one out of every five employed white men is skilled. Clerical occupations take 30 per cent of the employed white female workers but only 4 per cent of the Negro females employed. Female domestic servants are 4 per cent of the white female employment while over 40 per cent of the employed Negro females are in such service. The relatively high proportion of Negro females employed in professional and technical work (5.6 per cent) as compared with white females in similar work (13.2 per cent) is due in part to the number of Negro female teachers in the segregated schools of the South. If one compares Negro income with that of whites, the inferior position of the former is striking: less than one-half of the whites in the United States have incomes under $2,000, but nearly four-fifths of the Negroes are in this category; one out of every seven whites has an income over $4,000 but only one out of seventy Negroes has such an income. (The median incomes of Negroes in the North and West are 50 per cent higher than in the South—evidence of the impact of two world wars on the economic position of the Negro.)

ᴘᴏ *The American Negro and Politics.* In certain parts of the country, the political position of the American Negro has undergone an equally striking change. Negro participation in political life was not a problem or an issue during the period of slavery. With the end of the Civil War, however, it became a leading issue of great importance; the Negro was enfranchised. However, the end of the Reconstruction Era gave rise, in the South, to new limits on Negroes. Disenfranchisement took place and a system of legal segregation was established; the mark of inferior status was placed upon them.

The shift in Negro population to the northern cities and the increased economic opportunity led to a new era in Negro participation in political life and to a growing importance of political factors in race relations. The role of Negroes in the Republican and Democratic political machines is of acknowledged significance. Their influence has contributed to local, state, and national legislation on matters of discrimination in occupations, schools, and voting; the Supreme Court, through its decisions, has recognized inequality to be a violation of the American Creed in a number of important cases.

The American Negro's Social World. Along with the very fundamental changes in the political and economic life of the American Negro occurred equally basic changes in his social organization. These changes reflect a continuing shift in the nature or character of race relations and race attitudes in the United States. Originally, the Negroes' social world was defined in terms of the plantation system of which he was a basic part, and the race relations which developed in this system had a profound effect on the character of Negro society. The plantation system had its own social controls, traditions, and customs which regulated the form and extent of relationships between whites and Negroes. A division of labor resulted in the differential treatment of slaves, house servants occupying the highest rung. Skilled craftsmen were higher than the field hands.

Two aspects of the system were important in terms of race relations. First, "channels" were developed which transmitted some of the European culture of the masters to the household servants and the craftsmen. Second, the plantation system provided a pattern of personal relationships between whites and Negroes which persisted for many generations.

The period of emancipation and reconstruction shattered the plantation social system. Separate Negro communities developed, symbolic of their social status and "isolation." As part of a response to these developments, Negro associations, Negro churches, and Negro mutual societies came into being which reflected the particular outlook and folk traditions of the Negroes. Legalized separation continued to accentuate their differences.

The whole system of segregation in the South affected the southern public school system. Unlike the North, where the public schools played a fundamental role in the "melting pot," the segregated southern school proved to be a massive barrier to mutual understanding and the development of a common community life. In the South, the Negro's status was inferior in law and practice. The denial of adequate common, and therefore equal, educational services left a deep impress on Negro life and values, and it perpetuated two social worlds, one white, the other Negro. The relative absence of institutions of higher learning placed a further barrier against his assimilation. While barriers have been progressively reduced as a result of time and changes in attitude, and with the greater participation of Negroes in community life and affairs in the North and West, they still remain important in many areas of the South.

Several factors have facilitated changes in attitude toward the Negro in the United States. The challenge of Communism and its repeated emphasis on racial equality has had some effect. An obvious and pressing need for better race relations in the United States has risen in part from a fuller appreciation of our world position. The armed forces have played an important part. As a matter of public policy, and in the interest of battle efficiency, training, and economy,

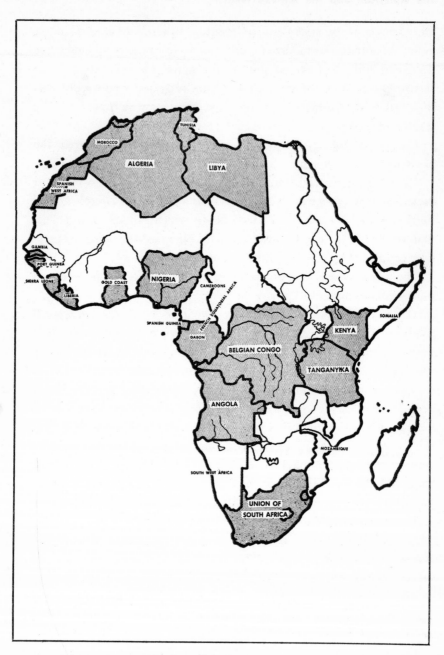

A. Areas of Tension in Africa

the segregation of troops has been gradually dispensed with. Large industrial organizations have also played a part, with increased needs for labor and the obvious impracticality of segregation on an assembly line. The process of labor unionization, with the integration of Negroes and poor whites, has been another force. A conference member noted that these forces making for change have resulted from special interests which have proved to be more important and pervasive than specific "facts" or attitudes on race itself.

One concluding observation that must be made in regard to the Negro and the problem of race relations in the United States is that there is now taking place on a wide front a reconciliation of the racial pattern with the American creed. The emphasis is on change— change in the Negro's economic status, community participation, and political life. *The direction of change is in the enlargement of freedom.* The speed, extent, and acceptance of this change varies widely, but it appeared to Negro conference members to be in part the result of the striking shifts which have occurred in the economic life and patterns of the United States within the last few generations. As such, these changes form one of the largest and most important fields of study in race relations today.

The African Negro

Southern Africa and Race. African race relations occupied a large part of the conference discussions. This was due in part to the great differences in the origin and development of race situations in the several areas reported. The conference interest also reflected public concern over race policies and tensions which have gained international significance. In the case of the American Negro, several conference members emphasized fundamental economic, political, and social changes which had had an undeniable effect on the position of the Negro. In the Near East, the ideological impact of modern European nationalism has been as much of a factor in race relations as sweeping economic and social change.

Generally speaking, African race relations are illustrative of those problems derived from the twin impact of economic change and political challenges arising partly from it and partly from a growing awareness of ideas of political freedom.

The history of African-European contact has only rarely been destructive of indigenous peoples or assimilative by gradual intermarriage. Rather, the history has been one of race division—division based on color and physical characteristics which play a primary part in determining one's social, economic, and political position. This is true of the greater part of Africa and explains why the question of race looms so large. However, the picture is not one of unrelieved gloom. It was clear to conference members that while there is a sense of great urgency with respect to most areas in which race is a problem, there are territories of West Africa, and individuals and institutions in other regions, including the Union of South Africa, which have a great interest in discovering a formula or way of life which will permit all peoples to play their part in the future of the continent.

In discussing race in Africa, a British scholar emphasized the extreme variations in the origin and development of human relations; these variations have resulted in different conceptions and attitudes toward race and different methods of control with different ends in view. While racial divisions and problems in southern Africa usually include four groups—whites, Asians (primarily Indians), blacks, and "mixed" or "colored"—the basic issue is the relations between whites and blacks. Variations in these relations apparently depend on the number of whites involved, the permanence of their stay, and the character of the economic stakes they have in the land. In South Africa, the ratio of whites to Bantus is 1 to 32; in Nyasaland 1 to 584. In those parts of Africa where the number of Europeans is small and the whites have no permanent stake (for example, Nigeria, Uganda, and the Gold Coast), race relations are markedly different from those in areas where the whites have a permanent stake (Union of South Africa, the Portuguese territories, and Kenya) which frequently conflicts with black African interests.

For much of Africa, contact began with a "foreign-policy" phase, during which the extension of European influence took the form of treaties, agreements, and contracts with tribal authorities. It also took the form of military alliances between Europeans and Africans, often directed against other Africans or Europeans. The second period was usually one of either white settlement outward of the areas of European administrative control into parts controlled by African Negroes or the extension of the boundaries of white control beyond the area of initial white settlement. In this latter extension, the natives continued their own lives but were governed by a white administrative bureaucracy. In the third phase, Africans and whites became separate parts of a single system in which the status and role of each were distinct and reserved. In this last phase, the difference between urban and rural areas and the conflict of economic interests which wish either to maintain a rural African labor supply or develop an urban one are of particular significance in the study of African race relations. The effects of such divisions are marked in the political views of each group. In this last phase may also come persistent attempts—such as in Kenya and the Union—to "freeze" the positions of natives and Europeans and to develop what sometimes appears to be a kind of caste system in which one's mode of life and community and political activity are determined primarily by one's color. The futility (apart from morality) of such attempts appears clear to observers when one appreciates the deep-seated changes occurring among the African Negroes through European contacts. The base of African society is changing perceptibly; it is patently not a foundation on which a durable, developing, and democratic society can be based if one group (white) attempts to determine the permanent status of others (black, Asian, and "colored" or "mixed").

The Black African and White European. The relationships between whites and Negroes have been described in economic, political, social, psuedobiological, and theological terms. The dominant problem and the theme of Africa is the growing extent to which African Negroes are challenging the position of whites. As the

Africans have more contact with whites and with each other, as they learn the technology and organizational skill of the Europeans, and begin to accept as their own the concepts of freedom defined by the West, their aspirations and sense of human dignity and equality will rise. Southern Africa is one of the most critical examples of the largely negative response of the white European to this unmistakable and irrepressible challenge from black Africa. It is a response which has yet to give any indication of resolving issues and lessening tensions. No matter what policy is chosen by the whites to resolve the conflicts of power and interest, it will be foredoomed to failure unless the formula is acceptable to the Negro.

From the point of view of both African Negroes and Europeans, population numbers and growth are of the greatest significance: the politically and economically dominant white element today is losing in population growth. Non-Europeans, including black Africans, Asians (chiefly Indians), and "mixed," outnumber Europeans four to one. Since the white dominant group has no intention of extending the franchise to give greater voice to the non-Europeans, the question of control passing slowly to them in a democratic manner does not arise. Hence the question of internal stability and law and order is very real.

A second factor of basic importance to race attitudes in the Union is the striking economic change which is occurring. The process of industrialization and urbanization is having a major effect on white-black relations. The Industrial Revolution has come to South Africa. Increased demands for workers means more Africans are entering the ranks of trained labor and competing increasingly with the lower-paid whites; more are moving permanently from village areas into cities; their organization is improving and they are becoming a consumer market of growing value. Africans are also becoming better educated and an educated elite is growing and spreading.

In 1946, the working population of the Union consisted of about 15 per cent Europeans, 6 per cent "colored," 2 per cent Asiatics, and 77 per cent Africans. In farming, forestry, and fishing, over 90 per

cent of the laborers were Negro. In mining and quarrying, about 88
per cent of the labor was African. Manufacturing, third in the scale,
has half of its labor force from the Africans. Most striking are the
percentage increases in African labor in certain occupations. In the
decade 1936–1946 there was a 2.2 per cent increase in the number of
Africans in farming and an 8.6 per cent increase in mining, but a 75
per cent increase in manufacturing, a 29 per cent in transport and
communications, an 86.2 per cent in commerce and finance, and
88.1 per cent in professions, entertainment, etc. These percentage
increases are important, but further evidence shows that some 83 per
cent of the African employees are still unskilled and only 4 per cent
are rated as skilled; contrast this with the unskilled European labor
(2 per cent) and skilled (83 per cent).

In education, considering the total number of children attending
schools, there were in 1951 about 540,000 Europeans, 213,000
"mixed," and 800,000 Africans. In the same year there were some
20,000 teachers in schools for Europeans and about 19,000 teachers
for Africans. In the year 1951–1952, four times as much was spent
on schools for Europeans as was spent on schools for Africans. In
that year there were over 18,000 Europeans in universities, but only
494 Africans.

The purpose of citing these figures is to indicate the tragic gap
that exists between the African Negro and the white. The figures on
education alone are a guide-marker to the future. It is incontestable
that the African's awareness of his position is growing rapidly.
Political consciousness in Africa, as in many other areas of the world,
is outdistancing needed reforms. The nature of the response of South
African whites to this rapidly developing situation is important.

The Place of the Black African. The several plans which
have been brought forward to resolve the crisis reflect the historical
setting of the racial groups concerned and the nature and extent of
their stake in the Union. The Afrikaners travelled to South Africa
to preserve their religious freedom and independence. At various
times battles were fought against the Hottentots, the Bushmen, and

the British. The Great Trek started at the beginning of the nineteenth century in response to repeated British efforts to introduce principles of racial equality and culminated in a struggle for the Transvaal gold fields. But today, "fifty years after their defeat in war, the most uncompromising champions of Afrikanerdom, its language, culture, and tradition, hold the reins of power and seek to abolish the last remnants of British power—the Crown and the British flag. The Afrikaners know no other home, no other allegiance, and today they are faced with a new threatened domination, that of the nonwhite peoples of the country. . . ." Descendants of British settlers have larger loyalties. Loyal to the Union, they sense and value the greater unity of the Commonwealth. To them, the British connection is worth preserving.

To the African Negro, the history of the Union is one of conquest, control, and exploitation. While some have benefited from the government, the vast majority believe the white man is determined to use every means to ensure his supremacy by laws, regulations, and policies designed to divide and segregate the African people.

The policies suggested by whites for handling the race issue for the future of the Union fall into three major groups. The first seeks total segregation and isolation, allowing each group to pursue its free and separate development. The second is "Apartheid," by which a limited and controlled number of Africans would work and live in white areas but the majority would live in the "reserves" where they would be assisted, but political power would rest with the whites. The third policy is that of "integration" in which the future of the Union would be increasingly one of black and white together. Here total assimilation of one by the other is not the goal; there is a conviction that within the framework of a democratic society each racial group should be able to develop and participate in a common national life.

Total Segregation. As described by a South African, the policy of total segregation implies permanent and separate residential areas for the Bantu population. These areas will constitute "national and political homes." One view in support of this policy concludes that since the Bantu will never be equal to the whites, it is more intelligent to separate the two than to force the Bantu "to be satisfied with such a state of affairs" which would lead to the "greatest disillusionment and strife." No one should expect the Bantu, so the argument runs, to be content unless he rules himself and this can be accomplished only by total territorial separation. This is deemed true because the numerical preponderance of Africans is clear and irrefutable, while "Europeans will never allow their political domination to be threatened and will never permit the African population to deprive them (Europeans) of their right of political self-determination."

If "integration" were to be accepted as a policy, the moment would necessarily come when, in order to preserve their rights and position, the whites would have to take steps to oppress the Africans. Since such a move would be unwelcome to both Negroes and whites, "the only just policy for all is territorial separation of Europeans and Africans." This separation would be achieved over a long period of time and would require the fullest possible economic development of African native reserves. Eventually all African Negroes would reside there except for a very few migrant workers whose permanent home would be in the reserves. The European would have no political rights in the Africans' areas and vice versa. Two other views, which support total segregation, suggest that the African will be able to attain full development and realize his own dignity and worth only when he is free to develop and assume responsibilities in his own country. The other view holds that the European can be saved from his own degeneration only by being compelled to abandon his control and exploitation of the African.

Apartheid. "Apartheid" stems from total segregation but differs importantly. Its supporters agree that black Africans outnumber Europeans and that "integration" will lead only to the disappearance of the white man and his civilzation. But "total segregation," which would have been possible several hundred years ago, is impractical today. Today, however, limited segregation offers a solution. Under this plan, a limited number of Africans would live and work in "European areas" but the majority would be in the reserves. By A.D. 2000 there would be no more than four million or so Africans working in the rural European areas; there would be some two to three million in the urban European areas. In the African areas there would be some twelve million. Many of these would work in adjacent areas, since the reserves could probably not be developed adequately to maintain the required millions. (In 1946, some 23 per cent of the Africans were in urban areas and some 39 per cent in native areas and 38 per cent in rural areas other than native areas. A key problem to Apartheid advocates is how to maintain this division at a time of economic and population growth; of how to continually relegate numbers of Africans to the reserves.)

Apartheid is the official policy of the Union government; it is implemented by a series of steps designed to prevent, for example, mixed marriages, to ensure the segregation of residential and business areas. (This will affect the "mixed" and Indian groups severely. The government pursues a policy which regards Indians as unassimilable as well.) Furthermore, the Union government is taking steps for the setting up or enlarging of government control over the African reserves and the separation of trade-unions on a color basis. A fixed contribution toward the cost of Bantu education is planned, the remainder being raised by the Africans themselves. There is a Public Amenities Act which makes it legal for public authorities and others to provide facilities for nonwhites not equal to those for whites. A South African (white) conference member, in response to a question, assured the conference that the Union government was confident it has the co-operation of Africans in these measures. In reply to another question as to whether there was an implied inferiority of the African Negro in Apartheid, he replied, no. Several suggested that recent developments in the United States and Hawaii indicated integration was possible, although the different setting was acknowledged. The reply was to the effect that historical forces in the Union made integration impossible. The conference was reminded by an African Negro that in his data paper he had warned against the appeal to history; that, as Professor Z. K. Matthews had once said, it is easy to "convince oneself that to account for a thing 'historically' provides a kind of moral justification for the thing itself."

The practicality of Apartheid in urban areas at a time of extensive industrial growth was raised by an American. It implies a stable labor force, but 750,000 Africans now in the Union have migrated from Basutoland. The Union's growing labor demands have, in effect, siphoned off the population increase of Basutoland. The suggestion was made that economic development and the discovery and exploitation of resources cannot be charted to such an extent as to make permanent planning of native areas feasible. How flexible can the location of such areas be?

African Integration. The South African Institute of Race Relations, English-speaking churches, and nonwhite political organizations advocate the third policy—"integration." They agree that total segregation is now impossible and base their policy "on the value of the individual and his right to the fullest expression and development in a democratic state with its accepted freedom, rights, and duties." They look to a time when South Africa will be a "multiracial" society. The native areas must be developed as rapidly as possible; migrant labor should be eliminated; the urbanization of nonwhites accepted, greater use made of aptitudes and skills of nonwhites, and free primary education and increased higher education provided. African trade-unions should be recognized, "pass" laws abolished, and a qualified franchise established for Africans on a common roll. Advocates of integration believe that established patterns of segregation will continue but that adjustments can be made as the system breaks down; any other approach will lead only to racial strife.

Several African Negroes at the conference gave their reactions to these views. They noted the response of their people, along with

those of the Indians in several cases, to the measures being considered
or passed by the Union government. The policy of Apartheid was
rejected unequivocally; in the interest of common welfare, African
Negroes seek an association with whites. Far from Apartheid re-
ducing areas of conflict, it increases the chance of it, for it implies
frustration of Africans at every point; other ethnic groups, numerically more important than the whites, have a right to determine
the future pattern of relationships. "It seems to us that . . . Apartheid, as a policy, is meant to benefit only the white man, and even its
most ardent theoreticians know that the politician and the average
Afrikaner farmer who support Apartheid do not do so because of
their love of the black man and his culture, but because it keeps the
black man 'in his place.' " Integration, with its concept of temporary
trusteeship, is acceptable to Africans. There is every danger that if
this view does not prevail, lines will be drawn and the explosion
of black African nationalism will follow.

Race in Central Africa

Central Africa is composed of nonself-governing territories
controlled by Great Britain, France, Portugal, and Belgium. Throughout this area, the white man is a distinct minority. Differences from
one area to another arise in part from the particular form of exploitation of the human and material resources of the region. Some variations are due to factors antedating the arrival of the white man.

Portuguese Africa. The Portuguese territories, Angola on
the west coast and Mozambique on the east, have had settlements
for more than four centuries, but effective control over the interior
was not achieved until the last century. The striking economic
changes planned and under way for the Congo, the Rhodesias, and
Nyasaland have not appeared in the Portuguese areas, partly because of the relative poverty of Portugal and partly because the distribution of power has been essentially unchanged during these centuries. The impulse for political and economic progress has not been
experienced as much here as elsewhere.

The pattern of race relations remains as it has been for several hundred years. The controlling group is not entirely "white," but contains some mixed, while the mass of the people are black. This is due to the partial assimilation of the offspring of marriages between Africans and Portuguese settlers. The ending of the slave trade around 1900 did not affect the traditional hierarchy, and today the "bulk of the population, which is black, remains poor and unenfranchised, while the elite, which governs the country and has a high position in industry and commerce, contains some people of all shades of color."

The Central African Federation and the Congo. The Belgian and British territories of Central Africa are substantially different from the Portuguese possessions. Industrial development and plantation agriculture have taken place. The Belgian Congo is, however, distinct from the Rhodesias in that it has been administered directly by Belgians for the benefit of the mother country. The interests of Belgium required a stable African urban population with growing knowledge of skills and no political power. Belgians who worked in the Congo maintained home ties; the children returned to Belgium for school and the men returned there on retirement. Practically no mixed marriages were recognized. The interest of the government lay in the long-range, intensive exploitation of resources, and political power has been granted neither to resident Belgians nor to the Africans. The second world war changed some aspects. Some of the men who were cut off from contact with Belgium came to regard the Congo as their home and actively sought political power. Tension is growing between them and the growing class of skilled Africans. Race divisions have been more sharply drawn than in the Portuguese territories, but there is greater occupational mobility and economic opportunity for Africans. As a result of the growing significance in the Congo, these Belgians settled in the colony seek close relationship with the English in the Rhodesias, who face somewhat similar problems. In their turn, African Negroes continue to seek greater opportunities and rely necessarily on the Belgian administration for protection against the views and aims of the settlers.

A significant difference between the Congo and the Rhodesias is that political control in the latter has already passed to the resident whites. The color line is drawn sharply (many of the white colonists in the Rhodesias came from the Union). Before the whites settled in Rhodesia, Africans were organized in fairly small tribal groups without much technical skill and no developed system of trade. In the eighteenth and nineteenth centuries these tribes were drawn into the slave trade and wars but were no match for the white forces. With little of the required skills, they did not participate in the development of their country; they entered the whites' economy as unskilled laborers and have had no place in the political system. Migrant labor was characteristic of the area, with Africans moving only temporarily, sometimes seasonally, from their homes to their wage-earning occupations. The growth of a permanent, urban African labor force was discouraged. Furthermore, the white settlers, unlike the Belgians of the Congo, gained substantial political power after World War I, with a consequent loss in control from London.

Several other factors have made Central Africa different from other regions. First, to date, the African has retained, by and large, much of his land, with white exploitation not taking the form of extensive plantation tracts and estates. There is no serious rural-squatter or tenantry problem. Most Africans in Northern Rhodesia and Nyasaland still have roots in the land. This has meant that Africans have preserved some of their own society and have been in a stronger position to accommodate themselves to changes resulting from the intrusion of the whites. This process has been facilitated by the British colonial policy of indirect rule, which has used traditional forms of social organization to achieve British purposes. Great changes have taken place in their society, but the African has had a measure of social continuity and, therefore, a degree of unity.

Today, there is a basic conflict between the Africans, the white settlers, and the administration over the future development of the

territories and the role each people will play. The settlers' interests
are increasingly concerned with the land, while some large companies and the administration seek to develop Africans in the rural
areas, at the same time retaining the system of migratory labor. This
is, again, a situation in which the issue of race is bound to become
more serious as the different and competing economic interests of
Europeans and African Negroes continue to develop unreconciled.

Race in British East and West Africa

British East Africa—Uganda, Kenya, and Tanganyika—
differs in many respects from the Portuguese and British territories
of Central Africa. In Uganda, the few whites (4,000 compared to
5,000,000 blacks) are mostly missionaries and government servants;
they have no permanent economic interest in the area. Race relations
in Uganda are, therefore, less tense and all-embracing than in neigh-
boring Kenya, where there is a relatively large, economically and
politically dominant white settler group numbering some 35,000.
Indians (100,000) form a middle trading group, as they do in
Uganda, with 5,000,000 Africans representing the subordinate
people.

Again, the problem of race is bound up intimately with that of
land. The highlands, which include most of the desirable land of
Kenya, has been divided largely among the white settlers who have
often reserved for the African's use, ostensibly for his "protection,"
submarginal and desert land. Not all the whites are farmers, but
those who are have large tracts of land and are dependent for labor
on Africans willing to move off the reserves. The disproportionate
share of good land acquired by white settlers underlies most of the
grave and continuing difficulties of Kenya, but various discriminatory
practices also have contributed to the economic and political frustrations of that land.

Nigeria and the Gold Coast have unique race situations which
have developed partly out of the special economic and political relationships between blacks and whites. Of the greatest significance,

however, is the remarkable process of cultural change which has been largely responsible for impressive political achievements.

At the time of first British contact, many of the peoples of the areas were illiterate and tribally primitive, with a subsistence-level economy, though there were also several powerful and wealthy kingdoms with highly developed cultures. Their conditions remained largely the same until the end of the nineteenth century, when change began and has continued to the present. In Nigeria and the Gold Coast, relationships between groups were described by several members as having no large racial content, although there is not complete intermixing, owing, as they described it, to their distinctly different cultural backgrounds. The racial problem is not entirely absent, but it is not dominant, as in the Union of South Africa.

The variations in race situations and attitudes in Africa appear to depend significantly on the number of European residents and their objectives. In West Africa, in contrast to Kenya or the Union, the British resident has no permanent stake. He is there for a time, as a government servant, as a representative of a firm, or as a missionary. When his tour of duty is over, he leaves. No vested interest in land complicates his position vis-a-vis the blacks, as in the highlands of Kenya. (The lowly but ubiquitous mosquito has played a role: an African conference member stated that because unfavorable health conditions in West Africa made permanent European settlement particularly difficult, it had been said that the "mosquito saved the West African from the burden of the white man.") Furthermore, the policy of the British government to grant freedom to the blacks has been consistent and, at the moment, practically achieved in the case of the Gold Coast. This relatively harmonious relationship between whites and blacks has led to a process of cultural adaptation rather than mere adjustment on the part of the blacks.

As a result of the introduction of Western techniques, education, and political and social organization, the Africans are developing a new society of their own. Progress in this adaptation or reconciliation of traditional tribal forms of society to the new has been uneven and is still restricted to a relatively small group. A large proportion of Africans continue to live in a tribal setting, with kinship a dominant feature of their lives. Many remain nonliterate, with attitudes conditioned by magico-religious beliefs in ancestral spirits and medicine. When one understands the extent of this tribal setting he appreciates better the dramatic story of the group which has emerged and on whose ability and cultural adaptation depends the future of its people as a modern nation. In summary, when considering the relatively favorable race relationships in West Africa one stresses the impermanent stake of British residents in contrast to the developing African consciousness of their future role. This relationship has been aided importantly by the political objectives set by the British government itself: freedom for West Africans.

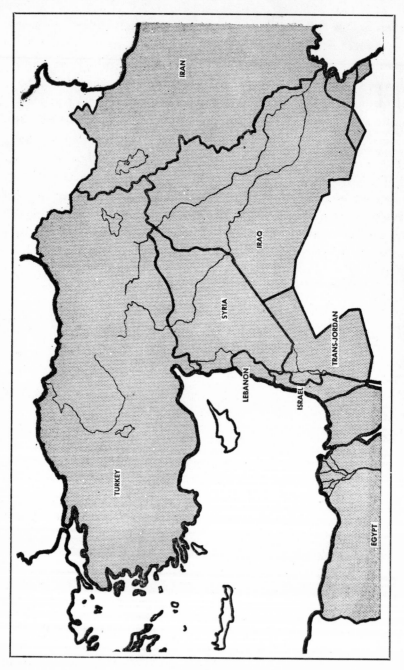

B. Areas of Tension in the Near East

Chapter 3

RACE SITUATIONS IN THE PACIFIC AND ASIA

Sources utilized in this chapter include, in addition to the conference reports and discussions, the following papers in Andrew W. Lind, ed., Race Relations in World Perspective *(Honolulu: University of Hawaii Press, 1955), "Race and Related Ideas in the Near East," by Albert Hourani, and "Race Relations in the Soviet Union," by Walter J. Kolarz.*

The Chinese and Malaya

Not all problems which may be defined as "racial" occur between whites and blacks or between Asians and Europeans. There have been repeated instances in history where relationships among Asian peoples themselves have taken on an appearance of "race." The persistent dislike of the Chinese in many areas of Southeast Asia has a strong element of race added to it, as have also the relationships between Hindus and Moslems. One should include in the Asian sphere the deep-seated, continuing problem of Russians and Central Asians. It is difficult to say whether, without the contribution of Western racism and concepts of race supremacy, one could properly ascribe feelings of race to the Asian groups involved in bitter issues of group relationships. The term "race" is used widely to focus attention on a situation; it has special symbolic and propaganda value and neatly sums up complex feelings about other people.

The Chinese Overseas. The reasons for Chinese migration to Southeast Asia are complicated. Most important originally were trade considerations and job opportunities open to them, particularly in the last century.

The problem of Chinese overseas stems from the fact that they invariably group themselves in organized communities which come to be regarded by the local peoples as "little Chinas." Insofar as possible, the Chinese have established their own schools, followed their own customs and beliefs, and married within their own community. They have retained close connections with their families in China, and have sent back considerable sums of money, whether they lived in Borneo or Burma, Thailand or Indo-China, Indonesia, Malaya, or the Philippines. A majority have engaged in business, an occupation not always held socially respectable in Southeast Asia. These communities have usually represented the most important commercial class—the middlemen—and have also been prominent in small rural towns, where the Chinese business store or factor is usually an important market for local produce and a major source of credit.

The interests of these overseas Chinese communities have been protected and served by stable political and economic conditions; they were never prominent in the nationalist, anti-colonial movements which swept Southeast Asia. But the Chinese have been deeply interested in politics at home. They have felt their security overseas dependent on a strong, nationalistic government in Peking. Chinese governments, mindful of the considerable foreign exchange remitted and the usefulness of "little Chinas" scattered through Southeast Asia, have reciprocated this interest and have maintained close political contact, paid for Chinese schools, run newspapers, started overseas branches of their particular political organizations, and interceded on occasion with other governments on matters affecting the welfare of their nationals overseas.

These factors, plus the history of Chinese imperial expansion into certain areas of Southeast Asia, have served to focus attention on these close-knit Chinese communities. The Chinese are generally regarded as not sharing the interests of the indigenous peoples. Their association with former colonial rulers makes them politically suspect, their commercial control is regarded as impeding economic development, and their social and cultural isolation is regarded as indicative of a refusal to participate in the development of a new national life in free areas of Southeast Asia.

Malaya: An Asian Race Situation. In most areas of Southeast Asia the Chinese communities are not large enough to constitute an important political community in relation to the rest of the population. But in Malaya, where nearly half the population is of Chinese origin, a unique situation has developed which has resulted in serious race problems affecting the political and economic future of that wealthy land. The Chinese dominate the economic life and have firm market control over a large part of agriculture and some of the mining and rubber. Chinese perform much of the mining and estate labor, while Malays are engaged largely in fishing and the cultivation of small agricultural holdings.

Political life in the Federation is dominated by Malays who regard the economic control by the Chinese as a constant threat to their control. Some of the Chinese fear an independent Malaya would result in damage to their economic interests. Since Chinese constitute a large part of the population, any significant extension of democratic rule would provoke a serious political crisis.

In a very real sense, and apart from their own important holdings, the British are able to remain in Malaya today because of the deep division between Chinese and Malays. Neither Chinese nor Malays can afford to see the British forced out until some accommodation is reached between the Asian groups. The situation is not static. Largely as a result of the guerrilla tactics of the Communists —made up overwhelmingly of those Chinese who are too poor to have a stake in the status quo and are supported quietly by those Chinese who think it best to ensure themselves against a possible future of Red rule—the British have sought to broaden and increase the Chinese stake in Malaya by greater Chinese participation in political life. This objective has been partly achieved through limited British success in making Malayan citizenship available to a larger number of Chinese who can meet residence, birth, and parentage qualifications. While these steps were believed necessary in view of the Communist campaigns and Communist appeals to Chinese, they were completed usually over the objections of the various Malay governments, who saw in Chinese support of the Communists further evidence of extraterritorial loyalty and interests and, in the new citizenship regulations, the beginning of Chinese political control. Under these circumstances, the Chinese and Malays express political views through parties which are usually racially exclusive. The Malays have their own organizations. While these groups do not resemble Western political parties, they are representative of important Malay and Chinese interests. The racial aspect of smoldering conflict is expressed by these exclusive organizations.

The future status of Singapore is of great importance in this setting of Chinese-Malay rivalry. More than 85 per cent of the great port's population is Chinese, and the city is the export channel for Malayan products to the outside world. Whether Singapore eventually becomes part of Malaya itself, or remains a separate entity as a British crown colony, it is certain that the economic life of Malaya will continue to be dominated by the port. Since its population is chiefly Chinese, they have great influence over the Peninsula.

More recently, Chinese-Malay conflicts have been symbolized, in part, in the field of education, especially in higher learning. The Chinese prefer to have their own school systems in Malaya as elsewhere in Southeast Asia. They prefer not to have Malay—or English—the only language spoken by the children. The University of Malaya was started to provide a common institution of higher learning in which both Malays and Chinese would be welcome. In practice, the Chinese assert, and the British deny, that the University has favored Malays. The Chinese charge, for example, that University language instruction provides no adequate opportunity for advanced study by Chinese students who have progressed through the Chinese school system. Furthermore, the suggested moving of the University from Singapore to the Federation symbolized to many Chinese the inadequacy of the center in terms of Chinese needs and interests. As a consequence of this dissatisfaction with the University program (and partly for political insurance), the Chinese have sent a large number of their students back to Communist China for advanced study.

Plans are now under way among the Chinese to develop their own institution, Nanyang University, to be located in Singapore. It was designed also to serve as a center to which students of overseas Chinese families from all over Southeast Asia will be sent rather than to centers in Communist China. While such an institution might prove useful, there is another purpose which is believed by some to be of equal importance in the minds of the founders: the creation of a university which will cater particularly to the needs of Chinese in Singapore and Malaya. If true, this will further divide the Chinese and the Malays. The Chinese resolve to proceed with the new university has been strengthened by British decisions to further the development of a national school system which would, in time, be the most important educational system, and would fuse Chinese and Malay elements, and lay the base of a Malayan society and nation. Many Chinese see in this scheme a threat to Chinese identity and accordingly oppose it; they sponsor the Chinese University as part of a continuing effort to preserve their separate life. This makes still more difficult any assimilation with Malays.

One of the other factors making assimilation policies more difficult is the relative absence of mixed marriages which would in themselves constitute a growing community less identified with either Malays or Chinese. The mixed marriages which have occurred have usually resulted in one of the partners passing over into the other's society. During the period of British encouragement of Chinese male labor, there was a considerable number of mixed marriages; but when the British encouraged the importation of Chinese females they may have been laying unconsciously the original base of the communal societies which divide Malaya today.

Malaya is an example of a developing racial problem of considerable danger to all parties involved. It is a somewhat novel situation in that the racial antagonism is not expressed in anti-white
terms alone or even importantly; it is defined largely in terms of
relationships between Asian groups kept under control by a continuation of European power—a power whose departure at this
moment would be regretted by Chinese and Malays alike. One thing
is certain. If the British intend to withdraw eventually from the
Malayan states, as they have indicated they will, the manner of their
going will be of the utmost importance. If the British utilize the
remainder of their stay in persistent efforts to keep the communal
societies together and foster common interests, the racial problem
will tend to disappear or at least become less explosive. If the British
find it necessary to leave abruptly as they did in Burma, Malaya will
experience extreme racial conflict. The potentialities of this situation
are well known to the Communist Chinese as the power of Peking
expands into Southeast Asia.

The Near East

Modern Nationalism and Race. It is evident from the
examples of the American and the African Negro that economic factors may be important in race situations. The overseas Chinese and the
Indians in Africa provide additional evidence of the importance of
economic forces in determining attitudes and trends in race relations.
Yet race problems and issues do not require an economic content;
their origin may lie in other directions. A British historian long
familiar with the Near East suggested that "modern racial tensions
are not the necessary consequence of the co-existence of races, but
rather of a certain modern idea about the function of races in political life." Tensions in the Near East today arise, in part, from the
racist base of the modern Western state—a concept "incompatible
with the principles on which the old Near Eastern community was
organized."

The history of the Near East characterizes the area as one of constant flux, a "world in movement." Throughout recorded history, the area has been a focus of nomadic peoples' wanderings, to the north and west out of the great Arabian peninsula or coming from the Central Asian region heading south or east into the more settled lands of the Near East. The nomads became settlers and, in turn, were followed by successive waves of other peoples. The great communication routes from Europe, Africa, and Asia crossing the Middle East were travelled by trade caravans and conquering armies, and by Christian pilgrimages to Jerusalem, and Moslem pilgrimages to Mecca and Medina. These movements brought about a complex mixture of peoples. In time, there developed three major groups united by folklore, customs, literature, ways of thought, and song: the Turkish, the Persian, and the Arabic.

These groups have had different historical and cultural experiences which have led, in part, to stresses and tensions within their societies. The rise of Islam, the growth and decline of the Ottoman Empire, and domination by Western powers are major phases in the history of the area. Each phase made its contribution to the problems and tensions between peoples of the Near East.

The Near East Communities. For more than four hundred years, the political community of the Near East has been Moslem. The Ottoman Empire was a religious state—an empire for Moslems. For the most part, differences between peoples within the Empire were described as religious. Even though Moslems formed the great majority of those in government, the separate religious groups of Christians, Jews, and other non-Moslems regulated their own communal life within their own "millets" or communities, which were recognized as such by the central government. The ecclesiastical head of each community was the recognized link to the center. "Membership of each group was defined by acceptance of its doctrinal basis, regardless of race or language: all the Jews of the Empire formed one "millet" whatever their provenance, and all the Orthodox formed one, "whether they were Greeks, Arabs, Rumanians, Bulgarians, or Serbs."

Fragmentation of Empire: Rise of Separatism and National-ism. This system was not static. Religious tensions between groups existed and, in time, the barriers between them became higher and of greater consequence. The religious communities acquired a "national" or ethnic significance as social ties and loyalties became stronger. But the separate communities were never wholly isolated because of the economic links which bound them together. There was a tendency for certain communities to perform particular jobs within the empire: merchants, financiers, and doctors tended to be Christians or Jews, while political and military posts were held by Moslems of the Balkans and Anatolia.

This system did not survive the shock of Western imperial rivalries and the weakening of Ottoman control from within as the communal system became ever more rigid and exclusive.

Western nationalism had a pervasive effect throughout the Near East. Nationalism swept the new rising classes, many of whose leaders received part or much of their education in Western institutions. Communal groups developed a political consciousness which led to a sense of nationhood and ethnic identity.

The Greek "millet" played an important part in spreading the concept of separate political existence. As the Greek example was taken up by others, a chain reaction ensued in which the Ottoman Empire was fractured and fragmented by religious, political, and ethnic differences.

The rapid growth of a Turkish nationalism from 1908 on hastened the collapse of the old Ottoman Empire. Under Kemal Ataturk, the modern Turkish state became a reality, with the remnants of empire achieving separate national identities of their own as Arab "nation-states." Non-Turkish elements were eliminated in large part from the Asia Minor core of new Turkey.

Religious links between some of the new national groups were dissolved, but within the new states the relationship between religion and ethnic origin persisted: citizens of new Turkey who were non-Moslems were discriminated against and in the Turkish-speaking

Greek church members were sent to, and welcomed in, Greece. The Arab nationalist movement has been more complex, in that continuing efforts were made by minority Christians and Western-educated Moslems to foster a nationalism in which religion would play no dominant part and in which the "Arab" identity would be based on long tradition, culture, and language, minus the religious qualification.

The Near East and the West. Onto the relationship of ethnic groups within the Near East, there has been grafted a no less tense and complex relationship between the Near Eastern peoples and those of the dominant West. On the purely political level, the relationship has depended on the attitude which the Western nations have taken toward the struggle for independence. The Balkan nations, having been freed by the help of the Western liberal powers, looked toward them with sympathy, and regarded with suspicion the powers of Central and Eastern Europe who still threatened their new liberty; the Turks, looking on the Western powers with suspicion as the real cause of their internal troubles, purged themselves of resentment by their complete victory in 1919–1923; the Arab peoples, willing to throw in their lot with Britain and France in World War I, acquired a still unpurged resentment when, at the end of the war, they were placed under British and French control; the Egyptians, struggling to free themselves of British domination, veered between suspicion of all Western powers and hopes that some rival of Britain would help them.

Behind these political attitudes there lay a feeling of inferiority, both in those material resources and skills which are necessary for survival in the modern world, and in the political virtues on which the greatness and stability of states depend. This sense of inferiority could lead, in those who were not steadied by cool reflection, to rejection of Western civilization, or to uncritical acceptance of it. It could lead, too, to a cynical oversubtlety of political explanation, a willingness to think not only of others but even of oneself as an instrument of Western purposes: a sense of being only the shadow of another's reality, which might have tragic results, as when a people was over-confident in pressing its claims upon another, in the belief that some Great Power would back it up. But there were individuals who kept clear of these errors, having achieved a balance based on reason and self-respect, moving easily in the present world but firmly rooted in their own past.

All such attitudes sprang from the feeling of the Near Eastern peoples that they lay not only under the power but under the judgment of the West; and it was not surprising that, faced with this lack of self-confidence, the judgment of the West should often be unfavorable, and should express itself in contempt—whether contempt for inferior peoples or for inferior cultures, whether open scorn at weakness and inefficiency, or the more subtle romantic liking for primitive peoples, so long as they do not disturb the pattern one is trying to impose. But mingled with this there was a sense of responsibility for those whose lives one had disturbed, and this, too, could show itself in many forms.

Other Near East Minorities. In the Near East, national tensions have been most acute "when certain conditions have been present: the embodiment of the national idea in independent nation-states; the presence of mixed populations; the growth of rival *bourgeoisies;* the persistence, behind the national feelings, of religious loyalties; the influence and rivalries of Great Powers. When all these conditions are present, the tension may issue in tragic disaster." These essential ingredients are found in the Turkish-Greek disaster of 1918–1922 and the Arab-Jewish conflict in Palestine.

While these examples are outstanding, largely because of the often tragic involvement of hundreds of thousands of people, there are other instances in which differences have not led and, according to the conference's Near East expert, probably will not lead, to open hostility. This is partly due to the relatively small size of the minorities concerned, and partly to the influence of Western liberal ideas, a sense of confidence in their own ability, and the existence of a common danger. The Kurdish people of the Near East are an example.

Turkey. The problem of the minority Kurds in Turkey, Iraq, and Syria remains important to each nation. In Turkey, the overwhelming majority of the people are both Turkish-speaking and Moslem. Some 7 per cent are Kurdish-speaking. Along with the Kurds, the Greeks, Armenians, and Jews comprise some 9 per cent of the population. The attitude of the government is consistent with its modern conception of the Turkish state: those that share the religion but are not Turkish by race are to be assimilated. Those that are not of the faith are, necessarily, foreigners. While the constitution provides for equal citizenship rights, the government has on occasion adopted discriminatory policies designed to serve the objectives of the state. Recently such acts have become less frequent, but non-Moslems, in particular, remain outside the national community. As the largest non-Turkish Moslem group, the Kurds have been a special problem and object of concern. Their location in the eastern and southern frontier zones, across which others of their people were living, accentuated their strategic weakness to modern Turkey. Abetted by a strong sense of a nationalism of their own, concerned over the direction and content of the modernizing policies of Ankara, Kurds have revolted unsuccessfully against the state on a number of occasions. In dealing with this minority problem, the government of Turkey has shifted Kurds around, tried to re-settle them, replaced tribal control by government administration, and improved communications, so as to extend the influence of the state into the more remote Kurdish regions. Some of these policies have been drastically executed, but the Kurdish problem has been only partially resolved and the Kurdish national idea persists.

Iraq. Iraq shares the Kurdish problem. The constitution recognizes equal rights and they have in general been upheld. The monarchy provides unity, and the continued presence of the British ensures continuity. The Kurds are too powerful, too organized, and too inaccessible to make any repression feasible. They are recognized as a separate element; in the north their language is used in law, administration, and primary schools. Most officials in the northern provinces are Kurds. There has been, however, marked reluctance on the part of this minority to accept governmental authority because of the spread of the national idea, tribal loyalties, and a past neglect of the outlying provinces on the part of the central government. It seems likely that with oil revenues this last consideration will become less important. The possibility remains, however, that the drive for Kurdish "autonomy" will perhaps be revived under Soviet inspiration (as occurred in 1946).

In the thirties, further minority trouble occurred between the government, Christians, and Assyrians. Tension has since diminished as a result of the resettlement of some of them. More important has been the Jewish problem. In 1948, there were some 150,000 Jews in Iraq who had become "Arabized." With the creation of Israel, their position became awkward. Jews had important economic roles; political antagonisms developed and the Iraq government became more unfriendly. "The new Israeli government spread among them the idea that they should constitute part of the Israeli nation. In 1950–1951 all but 10,000 left for Israel. The virtual disappearance of this ancient Jewish community showed clearly how the Western idea of nationalism could evoke hostility where it had not existed, and disrupt an age-old symbiosis."

Syria. Syria, with its overwhelmingly Arab population, contains some religious and ethnic minorities. Most of these are of no political significance; only the Kurds (250,000) and Armenians (100,000) have played political roles. The Kurds are less of a problem in Syria than in Iraq. They are scattered more widely throughout the country and, numerically speaking, are of less importance. Used in the past by the foreigners, especially the French, the Kurds were something of a danger to the state in the beginning. The Armenians as a whole have also adopted a more co-operative spirit and have chosen assimilation. The possibility of Soviet intrigue remains and was manifested in the postwar years when several thousand Armenians returned to the Armenian Soviet Republic.

Lebanon and Egypt. The Lebanese state is based on religious communities; the main tensions are religious, not ethnic. Two distinct groups, Armenian Orthodox and Armenian Catholics, have been problems in the past but are now increasingly part of Lebanese life. In Egypt, almost totally Arabic speaking, the only important minorities are found in the urban centers, "where a mixed European and Levantine middle class . . . has controlled the commercial and financial life of Egypt for almost a century." Their dominant position has been affected by a loss of legal privileges and foreign protection and has been challenged by the growth of an Egyptian merchant group.

Israel. Unlike other areas of the Near East, such as Lebanon, Israel has yet to define the role of religion and race in its national life. Israel's Christian and Moslem minorities total about 180,000, of which 35,000 are Christians. These minorities have been promised equality; they have their own organizations and participate to some extent in political life. Arabic is permitted in law, administration, parliament, and the schools. On the other hand, martial law reigns over most of the Arab districts, and there are restrictions on movement. Citizenship is open to Jews automatically and to others on certain conditions. Considerations of security and the national basis of the state are paramount in these acts rather than prejudice.

The Union of Soviet Socialist Republics: Central Asia

Communism and Race. Race relations could hardly have been discussed in world perspective at the conference without some reference to the attitudes and policies of the Russians and the international Communist movement. The impact of Communism has influenced undeniably the course of human relations in every area. Conference discussions included reports on two aspects: first, the race views of Russians within the Soviet Union, and second, race in reference to the international Communist movement iself.

According to a conference discussion leader, a former citizen of Czechoslovakia long familiar with the Soviet Union, the Russians have usually regarded problems of race with a spirit of tolerance. In recent centuries there has been a constant process of intermarriage between the peoples of European Russia so that "there arose a situation in Russia of which the French historian Rambaud said it would be absurd to reflect on the shade of brown or yellow of the skin, the greater or lesser angle at which the nose turns up, the degree of prominence of the cheek bones or the acuteness of slant of the eyes." The current Communist policy of race tolerance owes much to this long tradition of liberal Russian views.

Yet it is important to remember that the spirit of world toleration which animated many Russians is redirected in the Communist era by emphasis on the international class struggle as the determining characteristic of society; "racial differences have a real meaning for the orthodox Communist only insofar as they affect the development of class conflicts in a given society." This view may serve as the justification of policies of racial discrimination as well as of race toleration, depending upon the particular problem with which the Communist is concerned.

Despite this "practical" view of race relations, Communists have stressed abroad, and on many occasions at home, a doctrine of racial equality which has left a lasting impression on those Asians and Africans who have been deeply influenced by their experiences with whites. One has only to read the biographies of Asian leaders to learn of their reactions to a variety of acts of racial discrimination under European colonial rule, to appreciate the intensity of their experiences and the powerful emotional appeal Communist professions of race equality have had for them. This is not to say that all whites knew of or supported the racial attitudes which accompanied most European colonial rule. The recent history of colonial rule has not infrequently reflected the emerging consciousness of modern European man. Yet it is also a fact that, for the great majority of Asians, racial experiences with color lines occurred in areas dominated by white Europeans and not by Russians. It is also a fact that memories of exclusion from white social, political, and professional circles have persisted long after white control has disappeared. Insofar as exclusion was based on racial considerations, it affected directly the dignity of men, and memories of it remain to plague the West.

The Soviets have played upon these feelings in their propaganda. They have exploited "race" as an issue and as a symbol in South America, in the African areas, and in Southern and Eastern Asia. In the various nationalist movements, the theme of race has been emphasized again and again. Its use as a tactic in furthering Soviet programs has been apparent to outside observers and only sometimes by the peoples among whom it has been widely and frequently used. No greater evidence of the importance of race as a political issue is needed than its constant use by Communists. In using race as a weapon they are acknowledging the widespread interest in race problems and the deep emotional feelings involved.

In a sense, the Soviets have exploited as their own and for their own purposes the changing attitudes of Europeans which became important during the nineteenth and twentieth centuries. In effect, they turn the issue of race back on the European and focus it as an issue on the white man. There is an important undercurrent of race feeling and attitude which flows beneath the surface stream of political events in many parts of the world. Sometimes this force can be utilized and directed by skillful diversion, but it is not always controllable in the long run. The Soviet tactical use of race has already proved disadvantageous in relations with free nations. Here the Soviets are dealing with a force which can be and has been directed against themselves. Thus, when their policies call for opposition to the West and for subservience to Soviet views and leadership at the same time, Russian advisers and agents are likely to be regarded as symbols of Western colonization. The role of Communist "High Priests," which in the later years of Stalin's rule became the special province of European Russians, has caused difficulty among Central Asian nationalities as well as with satellites and others outside the borders of the U.S.S.R.

Race, as a factor in Soviet policy, is not always apparent. Political and economic policies within the U.S.S.R. may contain no suggestion or implication of race. In this context, the conference discussed primarily the relations between Great Russians and Central Asian nationalities as they have developed from Soviet policy and implementation.

Central Asia. The constitution of the Soviet Union recognizes the existence of heterogeneous groups of people in scattered areas of the U.S.S.R. by its provision for autonomous republics, provinces, and "national areas." These have been not permanent divisions but "time-serving" devices whose usefulness varies with national policy and developments. The Korean National District of the Soviet Far East has been abolished as have the republics of the Crimean Tartars, the Kalmucks, the Chechens and Ingushi, and the Autonomous Province of the Karachay. These disappeared because questions of loyalty were raised during the last war, and not because of any improvement in race relations which made the special divisions unnecessary. In many cases organized communities have been fragmented and the peoples deported to distant parts of the U.S.S.R. At one time the scheme of national collective farms was designed, in part, to provide a means for grouping relatively small numbers of peoples together, who became, as it were, "colonies" surrounded by ethnically different persons. "There existed such oddities as Baluchi National Collective Farms in Turkmenia, Kurdish National Farms in Armenia, Albania Collective Farms in the Ukraine, and an Estonian National Collective Farm in the Northern Caucasus." During and after the war many of these communities lost their separate status and ethnic distinctiveness in mergers which resulted for the most part in larger units incorporating ethnically diverse peoples.

Nationalism. Soviet policy and practice can be distinguished by such examples and also by the steps taken to discourage nationalist movements or tendencies on the part of minorities. While such moves have been frequently made by governments seeking to unify diverse peoples, the Soviet policies cannot be divorced from the oft-recurring political theme of Russian supremacy—the "elder-brother" concept—which has been of historic importance in the relationships between the "Russians" and their Southern and Central Asian and Far Eastern minorities.

From the earliest years of the Soviet Union, precautions have been taken to prevent association between ethnically diverse peoples. The governmental structure has been such as to put the ethnic groups in contact with the administrative center rather than with each other. Lines of communications within the U.S.S.R. resemble radii from the central government to different points without inter-connections.

The policy of "isolating" one group from another is character-istic of Communist treatment of the Oriental peoples of the Soviet Empire. Central Asia—a culturally and historically homogeneous region, was divided into six republics to fragment the Central Asian and Far Eastern peoples and make federation among them impos-sible. This effectively maintains the dominance of the Great Rus-sians. This dominance is justified by the Soviet concept of the Rus-sian "elder brother"—a "theory that makes inequality an official Soviet virtue."

The Great Russian People. While the position of the Great Russians was emphasized during World War II, their role in the development of the Soviet Union was actually underscored begin-ning in the thirties. At this time there began a deliberate infusion of Russian culture into Soviet history, art, and literature. Along with this drive to restore Russian culture was a determined effort to im-press on the minds of other ethnic peoples the obligations owed by them to the untiring and unsparing efforts of the Great Russians. The "elder-brother" position was described in the histories, songs, and poems of Asians. An example of this is in a poem by Rasul Gamzatov of the Avar tribe, quoted in the conference paper on the Soviet Union:

> You are our teacher in work, our defender in war; where necessary
>   you will help us, you will put things right!
> For all this we say, "thank you, thank you" to you.
> Oh! my friend. Oh! my Russian Comrade.

The paper referred also to a book published by A. Pankratova in 1952, *The Great Russian Nation,* which carried this theme to its ultimate expression. As summarized by a conference member the book told how:

> The Great Russian people have at all times made an unparalleled and un-selfish contribution to the economic and cultural development of all nation-alities which now inhabit the U.S.S.R. These, therefore, owe a debt of

gratitude to the Great Russians for the help and protection that has been extended to them, both in the Czarist past and in the Soviet present. In fact, they ought to be grateful even for having been conquered and annexed by Czarist Russia, for otherwise they might not have come into contact with the "advanced culture of the Russian people." It follows that anti-Russian uprisings which took place in the conquered territories in the nineteenth and the early twentieth centuries are *ipso facto* reactionary, for their leaders ignored the "progressive role" of Russian domination. Coming down to the Soviet period, it was the Russian people who formed the revolutionary vanguard in the difficult years in which the Communist regime was established. Later, the Russians led the industrialization and collectivization of the country. Also Stakhanov and the other great record-breakers on the labor front were Russians. During World War II the Russians were again the leaders. In the rear and at the front they were an example to the other nations in self-sacrifice and heroism. Out of the eleven thousand Soviet citizens who were awarded the title "Hero of the Soviet Union," nearly two-thirds were Russians, although the latter count for less than half of the entire population of the U.S.S.R.

The conference was reminded of an apparently contradictory policy of the Communists which has sometimes encouraged the study of Central Asian history and cultural achievements. In several cases this has been applied to backward, illiterate groups, and the Soviets have even invented a body of literature and a language. The policy of encouraging cultural expressions has been widely hailed by Soviets as evidence of their interest in preserving the best of indigenous cultures and their recognition of "equality." Discerning observers, however, believe this policy is not an end in itself but a step in the development and organization of nomadic and seminomadic peoples to a point where integration into the society of the Soviet Union is possible. At that time, indigenous cultures, invented or otherwise, are modified by the extensive process of Russianization which proceeds contemporaneously with political and economic action.

Russian Colonization. At the same time that the Soviets were emphasizing the role of the European Russians, economic development and colonization in the Central Asian and Far Eastern areas proceeded at a high rate. While the Soviets claim that the purpose of their extensive development programs is to raise the level of all peoples in the Soviet Union, along with this program has gone a large-scale colonizing effort in the Asian areas by peoples from European Russia. These peoples have been sent to perform managerial and engineering tasks, fill public administration jobs, and do manual labor. The introduction of European Russian peoples into these comparatively undeveloped areas is not of a temporary nature—the workers, managers, and engineers are now permanently located and have in many instances come to dominate the Central Asian peoples among whom they now live. This has been a conscious and necessary effort; the programs required large numbers of skilled Russians for purely practical reasons, but these reasons should not be regarded as the only ones which justified the policy of shifting large numbers of peoples to the new areas. The objectives of rapid development and effective political control were made possible by an extension of Russian influence into all aspects of Central Asian life. It extended the power of the Soviet government, and is one of the more significant means of evaluating the extent to which Soviet race policies recognize equality in a genuine sense. Or does the "elder-brother" view reflect the Orwell phrase that "some are more equal than others"?

The "European" colonization of Central Asian areas not only increased the population but also resulted in a rapid growth of cities and workers' towns, in an intensive exploitation of natural resources, and in a higher development of traditional agriculture and grazing. This, in turn, encouraged a greater degree of organization among the Asians themselves. Sample figures were quoted to illustrate the dominance of the "colonizers": in Kazakhstan in 1948, "the percentage of Kazakhs in five industrial ministries for which data were given was as follows: meat and dairy industry, 14 per cent; communal economy, 7.9 per cent; textile industry, 6.7 per cent; light industry, 4 per cent; local industry, 2 per cent." Again these figures reflect in part the less advanced cultural level of Kazakhs and their unfamiliarity with modern industrial and managerial tasks, but it also reflects the importance of the Russian element in a vital part

of their lives. While the dominance of this element is clear-cut, and
presumably permanent, in industries, it is less so in agricultural pur-
suits, where the Central Asian percentage is much higher. In political
affairs, the colonizers are of outstanding importance. " . . . the
European element plays a considerable role in the leading party
stratum in all Central Asian Republics, even in Uzbekistan, which
is far less colonized than either Kazakhastan or Kirghizia. At the
Eleventh Congress of the Uzbek Communist Party, held in September, 1952, as many as 31 per cent of the delegates were Russians,
and 10 per cent were Ukrainians, Jews, or other persons hailing
from European Russia. The Uzbeks themselves had a very narrow
majority of 52.8 per cent . . . ." It was apparent from conference
discussions that, while much less is heard of discrimination by the
Russian colonizers, it is as important a problem in the Soviet Union
as in other empires. It is one thing to direct economic development
and colonization to make the Soviet Union secure, and something
else to have this security take the form of an expansion of Russian
cultural, political, and economic influence, especially if that expansion generates disaffection and unrest because of the racial attitudes of the colonizers.

In the twenties and thirties, Russian expressions of supremacy
and discrimination in social activities and housing were labeled as
"great-power chauvinism," and repeated efforts were made to root
out these views by reports on discrimination publicized during the
purges. Since then no similar reports have been made public, but
certain trends are to be noted. They are part of the Russianization
movement already mentioned. For example, Central Asian universities are usually named after Russian rather than Asian leaders.
This pattern is followed in the naming of streets, parks, libraries,
institutes, and cities.

"A glance at the new map of Tadzhikistan shows to what extremes the
process of denationalization may go. Among the towns of Tadzhikistan,
there is now a Leninabad, a Kalininabad, a Voroshilovabad, a Kirovabad, a
Mikoyanabad, a Sovetabad, a Komsomolabad, and a Kolkhozabad. To realize the monstrosity of this new geographical terminology to the full, one

must remember that Tadzhikistan was the cradle of a very ancient civilization. The place which is now called Leninabad was previously Khodzhent and before that Alexandria Eschate. It was founded by Alexander the Great (356–323 B.C.).

The reaction of Asians to this process is necessarily a subtle one and has been expressed in boycotts of Russians and Russianized towns and in various ways through literature.

The place of Asians in the eyes of the colonizers should be viewed not only in its Central Asian context but also in the setting of Asian unskilled workers living in European Russia. The conference was informed that Asians live and work under decidedly inferior conditions and "constitute the very bottom of the Soviet industrial proletariat." Few from Central Asia have attained even a middle level of authority in the Central government; "no Central Asian has ever become a member of the Communist Politbureau, a key minister in the Central Government, the commander of a military district, or a department chief of the Central Committee." This is not to say that nationality groups within the U.S.S.R. have always been neglected, for certain areas have been favored from time to time, but it appears that important posts are reserved for European Russians and certain privileged minorities.

As a result of the "Russianization" of regions within the U.S.S.R. it seems apparent that many of the ethnic groups will steadily lose out, with some doomed to eventual extinction. While the weight of Russian influence seems preponderant, there are several factors which must be noted. The first is the comparative "immunity" of Central Asians to Communism itself. The urban proletariat emphasis of Soviet Communism is a limiting factor when applied to predominantly rural peoples. There is also the factor of religion; the Moslem influence is extensive among most indigenous Central Asians. Because of these factors the Soviets have made concessions on occasion in recognition of the special problems inherent in Central Asia. "On the whole, party membership in the Oriental Republics of the Soviet Union does not achieve the purpose of genuine ideological transformation which would destroy the national individuality of the native of Central Asia and make him a one-hundred-per-cent *Homo sovieticus.* In the more remote tribal territories—say, in Northern Siberia, or in certain mountain areas of the Caucasus—people were for a long time unaware of the Communist Party and even of the existence of Soviet power."

The Soviets are concerned about this problem and the recurrent nationalism which remains a partial antidote to Russianization policies. Periodic purges have rooted out many actual or potential leaders of a nationalistic revival. Expressions of nationalism are found in the writings of Central Asians and serve to remind the people of a glorious period of history prior to the coming of the Russians. National heroes of recent years are mentioned, especially those of the nineteenth century resistance movement against Russia. If nationalism cannot be expressed in political action, it remains an important, continuing idea in cultural fields. It is of more than passing interest that the Asian victims of the 1950–1953 purge were individuals, largely intellectuals, who were themselves brought up within the Soviet system. Despite this "orientation," Central Asian nationalism demonstrates its continuing vitality.

One effect of the Moslem faith has been to make unimportant the number of mixed marriages. Generally, when mixed marriages occur they are on Moslem terms. A recurrent theme in contemporary Kazakh literature is the capitulation of Russian Communists to Central Asian customs. Examples of this theme were cited in the conference document from a novel by Sabit Mukanov and a poem by Khalizhan Bekkhozhin. The former concerns an old Party man who makes concessions to an Oriental woman; the latter treats of a Russian girl who gives up her customs and language and marries a Kazakh, the marriage being justified by the remark "nothing Russian is left in Mary's soul." Both novelist and poet have been denounced "for perverting the idea of Kazakh-Russian friendship."

So the future of the peoples of Russia seems to depend very largely on the result of a great sociological race. Which will win it—the economic, cultural, and general policy of the Russian Communist regime, which has the effect of obliterating the national characteristics of the racial groups of the U.S.S.R., or the national traditions and values of the pre-Communist era? Seen within an exclusively terrestrial and materialistic horizon, the two competitors participating in the race may seem to be as unequal as a column of armored cars and a herd of camels. But it is by no means a foregone conclusion that victory will be with a force which at a superficial glance seems to be physically stronger. . . .

The final triumph of Soviet policy on race relations is far from certain, even if viewed in total isolation from anything that takes place in the non-Communist world. The ambitions of the Communist regime have been staked too high. In the long run it cannot go on forcing a diluted form of Russian and Slavonic civilization upon the unwilling peoples of Asia, while simultaneously oppressing the Russians and the other Slavs at home. The Communist regime, by imposing untold sufferings on Russians and non-Russians alike, has put the Russian people in a position where it might have to prove that there is a great deal more truth in the theory of of the Russian "elder brother" than we might be inclined to think at the present time, although not in the sense in which the theory has been formulated by Stalin or Mme. Pankratova.

Hawaii

All of the major factors contributing to race situations in the various areas discussed by conference members have been present in Hawaii. Economic, ideological, cultural, political, and social problems—described in terms of New World, Asian, and African race relations—are all found in the race relations of the Hawaiian Islands. All of the major changes observed in race situations are found, also, in the Hawaiian Islands: urbanization, industrialization, changes in political and economic control, effects of education, and evidence of cultural accommodation and adjustment. The Hawaiian Islands were discussed with special interest, insofar as the speed and character of these changes might indicate a "pattern" for other areas.

The conference sessions on Hawaii were devoted to reports from three scholars with long familiarity with race problems in the Islands. Their reports described the history of the Islands in terms of the coming of peoples of various races, their roles originally in Hawaii, and the changes which have affected them and which they have helped effect. Hawaii was considered an example of a "frontier"—

the area in which diverse peoples have their contacts, establish systems of relationships, and within which "new" peoples and societies emerge. In the history of Hawaii one can trace the influence of missionary, political, cultural, and social frontiers.

Population. An estimate of the number of Hawaiians in the Islands at the time of Captain James Cook's "discovery" is about 300,000. The decline in their number to 12,000 ("pure" Hawaiians) and the emergence of a population of mixed racial character (74,000) is one of the major themes in the history of race in Hawaii. Caucasians began arriving in the Islands about 1820 as missionaries and traders, and now number some 115,000. Other peoples began to arrive in the Islands shortly after, and for the next hundred years a stream of Chinese, Japanese, Okinawans, Filipinos, Portuguese, Negroes, Koreans, Indians, Spaniards, Russians, Puerto Ricans, Norwegians, and South Sea Islanders entered the Hawaiian community. Some 400,000, chiefly Filipinos, Chinese, and Japanese, were imported to work as laborers on the plantations, since Hawaiians were too few in number and were ill-adapted to plantation labor systems. The 1950 census reported 86,000 Hawaiians and Part-Hawaiians, 115,000 Caucasians, 32,000 Chinese, 61,000 Filipinos, 185,000 Japanese, 7,000 Koreans, 2,500 Negroes, 10,000 Puerto Ricans, and 1,500 "others." Those of Japanese origin account for 37 per cent, Caucasians 23 per cent, and Hawaiians 17 per cent; approximately half the population is of Oriental background.

Mixed marriages have always been important, owing to the high ratio of males among Chinese, Filipinos, and Koreans. (Issue of these marriages have been listed usually as Chinese, Korean, or Filipino and not as part Chinese, part Korean, part Filipino, or part Caucasian. There is a possible reflection of racial bias in this classification system and it is proving less satisfactory with time.) As of 1950, about 30 per cent of the children born in the Hawaiian Islands were racially mixed. The speed with which this melding is occurring is indicated by the fact that the "mixed" Hawaiian population increased by some 55 per cent in the decade 1940–1950.

The history of race in Hawaii is not one of each race or national group remaining a self-sufficient, self-isolated community. Hawaiian race history is one of initial differences within and between each racial or national group, with a general, persistent trend toward the dissolution of those differences. There is no communal society such as that which characterizes and is the tragedy of Malaya.

Ethnic Divisions and Assimilation. The Hawaiians divide themselves today on rural, urban, and island bases. In the past, during the monarchy, the emphasis was placed on one's nobility; the early Caucasians, or *haoles,* as a result of marrying early into the higher ranks, established for themselves a position of economic, political, and social supremacy that was maintained until the past several decades. These early Caucasians did not constitute a united front but were divided deeply, with British, Americans, French, and Germans frequently opposed to each other. However, the Caucasians were the "managerial" group and constituted thus an "upper class" for many generations until, largely during and as a result of World War II, large numbers of Caucasian defense workers were brought to the Islands. The Chinese were also a divided people. Distinctions were made on the basis of one's family, origin (the division being chiefly one of Punti and Hakka), and whether one's family was descended from a contract laborer brought to Hawaii or from one who migrated under other circumstances.

Among the Japanese there is a continuing division between Naichi and those of Okinawa. (In earlier times there was an important division within the Japanese, stemming from one's social status and background in Japan, a distinction being made between "Eta" and others.) Filipinos differentiate between Tagalogs, Visayans, and the more recent Ilocanos. These differences are based on one's origin; other differences have arisen on the basis of changes which have occurred within a group after residing in the Islands. Sometimes these differences are cultural, occupational, or residential. A small but rapidly growing professional class has become distinct from the shopkeepers and laborers. There have been divisions caused by acceptance of Christianity, subdivided still further by adherence to sects within the faith. Social institutions based on village origin, class societies, benevolent associations, guilds, and temple groups traditional in China and characteristic of overseas Chinese have again divided the Chinese; it is impossible to refer to the Chinese and those of Chinese origin as belonging to the cohesive Chinese "community." The divisions have themselves given way in part to new forms of organization patterned after Western ones: Chinese chambers of commerce, professional societies, university groups; and these, in turn, have tended to become part of interracial organizations and societies which include several or all racial groups and have a community-wide responsibility and purpose. This trend, which dissolves over a period of time the barriers between groups, has been facilitated and perhaps made possible by several factors: the missionary influence, the ideological backgrounds of the once dominant Caucasian groups, and the isolation of Hawaii for a number of generations from international political conflicts, which has permitted a relatively undisturbed development. Of greater importance, however, has been the plantation system as a "race-making" factor, the influence of Honolulu as an urban center close to the plantations without the customs and restrictions of the latter, and, finally, the extensive influence of the American public school system.

The importance of the plantation system cannot be denied; it was responsible for the importation of labor from many parts of the Pacific area; insofar as laborers tended to come mainly from China, Japan, and the Philippines at certain periods, and were housed in and worked in these groups, the plantation system itself became a race-making situation in which the Chinese, Japanese, and Filipinos gained conceptions of themselves they had not held before. While some modest efforts were made by plantations to bring the workers into closer association with Western ways and beliefs, the interests of the plantations were in the preservation of their labor force and not in change.

This attitude was changed abruptly as a result of extensive unionization, which also led in part to the decision to mechanize the plantations whenever and wherever possible. These two factors have contributed greatly to the breaking down of the isolating effect of the plantation systems.

The proximity of large urban centers, notably Honolulu, has been of prime importance in the development of race situations and race trends. Laborers imported to plantations drifted to the city once their contract period was completed; their children sought other work and, at an increasingly rapid rate, became small merchants and shopkeepers. The widespread acceptance of the market as a place in which racial considerations played a subordinate role to that of skill in business contributed greatly to a playing down of racial factors. The drift of laborers from the plantations brought ethnic groups into more frequent contact with each other and to a certain extent made them dependent on each other. All these forces shaped the interracial character of the communities of the Hawaiian Islands.

The greatest transformer has been the compulsory public school system. Here, children of every racial and national origin have for a number of years associated within a Western pattern. The language of instruction has been English, and the teaching of American history and English literature has had a profound unifying effect. The multitude of school societies which have taken much of the extracurricular time of students have given them a social environment and values which differ markedly in many cases from those of the home life.

The reaction of the Caucasians or *haoles* to these developments is of interest in view of the problems of race relationships involving Europeans and Orientals and Negroes in other areas of the world. There can be no question that for nearly a hundred years the dominant group in the Islands was the Caucasian one. In economic affairs they gained early and easily a position and interests which resulted in the annexation of the Islands by the United States. The overwhelming importance of sugar led to greater demands for labor than Hawaiians could or were willing to meet; hence, as we have seen, workers were imported. It would be impossible to characterize in any rigid form the reaction of *haoles* to subsequent developments. Certainly the drain of laborers to the city affected the plantations in a direct manner; certainly the growth of small-scale business enterprises conflicted with larger business interests of *haoles*. Insofar as the school system tended to break down existing relationships it might be said to have adversely affected some *haole* interests. Yet having said that, it is equally true and of greater significance that the *haoles* did support a public school system, did not make it impossible for labor to leave the plantations, and did not suppress the trend toward small business even though they have not gone out of their way to encourage it. In political affairs, it was to be expected that *haoles* would play an early, dominating role, but as all the racial and national groups have developed and changed they have played increasingly important roles. Today, the *haoles,* particularly those with Island associations stretching back many years, constitute an interest group, albeit an important, but no longer controlling, one. A measure of the extent to which political control is exercised now by American citizens of Oriental background is found in a report in the *Honolulu Star-Bulletin* of the legislature elected in November, 1954. Of the fifteen elected members of the senate, seven have Japanese names, two Chinese, four show a European, Hawaiian, or other background, and two are of Portuguese origin. The house of representatives with thirty members contains one whose name indicates a Philippine background, fourteen of Japanese origin, nine European, Hawaiian, or other, five Portuguese, and one of Korean origin. (There are no appointed members of either the senate or the house, nor are there seats reserved for minority representation.)

In the discussions on African race relations, emphasis was repeatedly placed on the nature of the white economic stake; race tensions appeared to be less in areas where there were no permanent white economic interests, where the whites were the missionaries and the civil servants. Conversely, a number of the conference members pointed out that where whites have established themselves permanently, as in Kenya and the Union, race issues are important, especially when the economic stake conflicts with the traditional interests of the indigenous people. Hawaii, by this interpretation, should have had serious race problems, for, while it has been dominated by a plantation system—which involved land—the managers and owners were also for the greatest part permanent residents. In the case of Hawaii the answer lies partly in the early loss of control by the native Hawaiians over the broad, flat acreage required by the plantations and partly in the large importation of new peoples whose interests for a time were necessarily involved in the plantation system. Other factors were the cultural background of the *haoles* (nineteenth century New England), their early relationship with the Hawaiians, and the general American influence which came to be supreme. Most important was the role of the commercial and trading influences which provided substitutes for land as the source of economic opportunity.

The influence of the American system provided an ideological and legal framework for society. This total setting provided both restraints and areas of freedom. The general acceptance of this by *haoles* did not and does not prevent them from viewing matters in terms of their interests as do other groups within the community; the important point is that the Hawaiian Islands have experienced a number of fundamental changes without periods of oppression by the Caucasians or *haoles* and without their having any privileged occupations or social position defined and sanctioned by law or theology.

This is not to say that race relations in the community are as good as is often reported, but neither are they as bad. The emphasis is necessarily placed on change; one can find evidence, for example, of racial qualifications for club membership, and restricted residential areas and political office. One can also discover the extent to which these have been steadily modified under the impact of urban centers, education, economic change, improvement of communications, labor organization, mixed marriages, two world wars, and tourism. Race relations in Hawaii cannot be analyzed successfully by any approach which neglects the dynamic factors operating throughout the society. It is in this sense that the Hawaiian Islands are a composite picture of race trends in many other regions. It may be that in one area of the world the economic factor appears to be the key, and in another the political or cultural factor, but all of these factors are operating in the Hawaiian scene.

Chapter 4

RESPONSE TO RACE SITUATIONS

Sources utilized in this chapter, in addition to conference reports and discussions, include the following paper in Andrew W. Lind, ed., Race Relations in World Perspective *(Honolulu: University of Hawaii Press, 1955): "Social Roles and Types in Race Relations," by Clarence E. Glick.*

The examples of race relations in the Soviet Union, the Near East, Africa, the United States, Southeast Asia, and Hawaii illustrate the complexity of race issues. These examples offer final proof, if additional proof is needed, that race and race relations cannot be defined in biological terms alone—race is more frequently, as one conference member described it, a matter of "social discovery."

In the discussions of conference members there was deep and continuing interest expressed in the influence racial ideas and racial experiences have on individuals and groups of people. What is the nature of their reaction? How interwoven in the fabric of modern political and ideological movements are strands of racism? What kinds of individuals emerge as leaders of new groups of peoples? What ideas and symbols become significant to them and their followers? These questions are important. Race issues have played a large part in modern political movements in Asia; they will be of even greater importance in Africa. Race has often played an important part in the reactions of peoples emerging from a tribal or nomadic state under the impact of Western technology, values, and modern communications. In conference discussions, emphasis was put on the patterns of race relations emerging in colonial areas and among new nations.

These patterns must be examined in the context of the sweeping ideological and political movements affecting hundreds of millions of black and brown peoples in the New World and in the Old; in areas stretching from Gibraltar to Cape Town; from West Africa through the Near East, India, and into Southeast Asia; from the Argentine to the United States. An American with many years of experience in Asia stressed that in these movements the element of race, and particularly Western racism, plays a profound part. As he expressed it "no one who has had any contact with the men who have made these movements can avoid knowing that they have been driven to act as they have in no small measure by their experience with Western racism. At all points along the political spectrum from conservative to radical, from democratic to autocratic, these men all show, directly or indirectly, the effects of life under a regime of enforced racial inferiority."

The speaker stressed the Asian and African identification of "white," not only with racist policy or racial experiences, but with imperialism itself; the white European stood not only for racial but for political and military superiority as well. As Asians and Africans became more knowledgeable in Western ways and were brought into the main stream of contemporary affairs, they became aware of weaknesses in the Western nations and learned also of the contradictions inherent in Western colonialism and Western political freedom. The reaction of these peoples has been complex and of great vigor. In order to trace the development of race problems, it proved useful to divide their historical experiences into several phases. In each, there occurred substantial changes in the nature and extent of intergroup relationships, and in each racism played an increasingly important role. A number of conference members suggested various ways of describing these historical experiences. All were based on the evolving character of Western colonialism and the extensive impact of the West on indigenous peoples.

Western Expansion, Indigenous Peoples, and Race

One member suggested that nationalism—and race— should be examined in terms of the historical experiences and responses of indigenous peoples coming under outside domination. Four phases were suggested: *precontact, contact* or *predomination, domination,* and the *contemporary* or *post-domination* period. Not all areas pass through the four phases. Some indigenous peoples, such as the American Indian, may be virtually annihilated in the initial contact. Others, such as the Australian aborigine, may pass through a phase of marked demographic decline almost to extinction, then respond to the challenge, increase in numbers, and again become important. There are other contemporary race situations in South America and in the United States which could not be studied by this historical method, for it examines race situations primarily in a colonial context. However, in view of the number and importance of race situations in colonial areas of the world, this historical emphasis is useful.

The first, or precontact, phase marks the period prior to European domination, when there were existing societies in many areas into which the white man entered. Some of these were of a tribal nature in which social customs and institutions affected a relatively small cohesive group, where there were no body of literature and no written histories or philosophies, and where tradition and concepts of common descent were the binding forces. This was markedly true of the black Africans into whose life the white Europeans intruded. But in other regions Western man found himself dealing with highly organized societies, partially literate, with historical and cultural records of great antiquity: Indonesia, Indo-China, Burma, India, and Ceylon. In studying the European impact upon these developed societies, one is impressed by their slow response to Western challenge. They seemed unable to adapt themselves and their institutions to new forces and ideas.

In Africa and in Asia the ubiquitous European commercial station represented the first permanent expression of Western interests.

Initially, at least, these outposts did not challenge native customs and institutions. With time, however, their influence grew, and the trading station became the outpost of empire. Since the European was far from home, many of the restraints his society placed upon him faded, and the peculiar "colonial type" emerged with a different set of values and standards. Important among these was the belief in one's racial superiority. This belief was sometimes coupled to, and reinforced by, a religious zeal in which the colonial's superior position seemed assured in view of the barbaric paganism of the peoples with whom he dealt. The natives were clearly inferior in culture and power, were different in so many ways from the European that a *racial* inferiority was the easiest explanation of these differences and the justification for them. Thus, the racial frontier was established early in this initial period of contact with Western man. The length of this period varied from region to region, depending upon the nature, interest, and power of the Western nation concerned, but no *system* of relationships between the indigenous peoples and the Westerners was established. It was more a period in which the indigenous peoples tried unsuccessfully to fit the Westerner into their societies and customs.

Inevitably, however, certain transformations occurred. If the European man found himself freer in his conduct than in Europe and evolving into a colonial type with certain beliefs about the native, some Asian or African leaders also found necessary some modification of their own customs and institutions so as to deal better with, or contain more effectively, Western power. New conceptions by the Western trader of himself and his conduct were paralleled by new conceptions by leaders of tribal and more developed native societies. In other cases where adjustment did not take place, conflicts with Western power led to the collapse of local power and influence, which was followed by continued Western expansion, as in Burma. Indigenous leadership often disintegrated, and the renaissance of native leadership had to await some new type better equipped to deal with the West. The emergence of such leadership did not occur to any significant extent until the third period—the one in which Western rule and institutions were extended for a variety of reasons usually related to the security of commercial interests.

The next phase, domination, covers that period in which indigenous control disappears and Western power becomes supreme. With domination, a pattern of relationships emerges which defines the status of the indigenous people and the rulers. It is usually a period in which native morale, institutions, and customs lose vigor, meaning, and usefulness. It has been Western mission experience, the conference was told, that the greatest number of religious conversions occur during this period, symbolizing one kind of native personal accommodation to a new, more powerful, and hence, desirable, characteristic of Western society.

With Western contact, a few natives begin to play the part of intermediaries between two different cultural worlds. Depending upon the situation, natives may find themselves eventually laboring in Western-controlled enterprises or in reserves where important decisions are made for them by European administrators; or the natives may find themselves in competition with the new rulers for land and resources with some natives managing to preserve for themselves a measure of social and economic freedom. Others gradually evolve into a group of low-level government personnel and civil servants whose status and standards of living depend no longer, even in part, on any acknowledgement by their fellow natives of their new status. These natives depend upon the Western rulers for their work, promotion, and security. Useful, and in time essential, to the rulers, they are fully aware they are not considered to be socially equal or, in most cases, even socially acceptable to their rulers. As the period of full Western control approaches, the economic exploitation of labor and resources continues, political control is increased, and this "social distance" between European and native is rigidly maintained despite the increasing number of natives who pass over and into the field of European service.

With Western domination a fact, the metropolitan power increases its role in colonial affairs and, depending upon circumstances, will either see its interests defined in terms of the colonial investments held by its citizens or may assume a middle position in which the government attemps to moderate between the interests of its people and the natives themselves (as has occurred in Kenya). Changes continue to develop within the native society itself, the process of acculturation having as its active agent the new culture of the ruler.

Those natives who are actively involved in the colonial society, on however low a level, react to the new culture most quickly and adapt themselves to as many of the forms as possible. They are the ones who emulate the practices and habits of the colonial rulers, and begin to acquire the techniques and the rudiments of Western education. As this process continues, the natives become increasingly isolated from their own people and yet are not assimilated into the dominant group. The native-in-transition is dependent upon the colonial society for his status and living; yet he is not part of the society, he has kept few roots from his past and has only an attenuated contact with his contemporaries, who retain most of the traditional values and customs. As the native learns more of the dominant society's culture—and this may come from educational systems introduced by that society—he becomes increasingly aware of the fact that his status, despite his efforts to acquire new skills and attitudes, "in the eyes of members of the dominant group, is not determined by his culture, his value system and style of life, but by his *race*" and "his race is identified by physical marks of visibility which no personal effort can erase."

This discovery on the part of the native leads to a series of reactions of fundamental importance. This discovery has a shattering effect on an individual which leaves a deep and permanent scar on his personality. It affects, inevitably, the character of indigenous leadership, the content of nationalist movements, and the form of expression used by natives to reassert their human dignity. Some manage to accept the knowledge of assumed racial inferiority as part of the system, others accept it in a spirit of humiliation. Still others recognize it as a challenge and rise to meet it. Race as an issue intrudes into every aspect of the communal relationship—in matters of labor, credit, education, communications, occupations, political and social roles, residential and institutional restrictions, and in the ideological war for the minds of men.

The final phase to be considered in terms of response is that of post-domination—the period in which dominant political control passes and the indigenous peoples assume responsibility for their own affairs. In this process, which may be peaceful as in the Gold Coast, or militant as in Indonesia, two movements develop within the communal framework. One is the force for integration—that of further and more widespread adaptation; the other is the nationalist movement expressing itself in political ends, economic objectives, using counter-racism in some form, and a revived interest in, and not infrequently a magnification of, traditional indigenous virtues. The occupations set aside by the European as reserved become symbols for the movement, and a racist emphasis in nationalist literature and propaganda provides an effective unifying force for the movement itself. In many nationalist movements, the forces and personalities involved are frequently of sectional interest only. The unifying aspect of a racist symbol is, therefore, of great importance and, along with the objective of freedom or self-determination, its use provides a key sense of *national unity*. The indigenous peoples gain new conceptions of themselves: they are no longer Shan or Chin peoples, they are now consciously *Burmans;* they are not Javanese only, they are *Indonesians.* This new-found national consciousness is posed against the British, the Dutch, or others; and *color* becomes symbolic of a host of complex feelings of frustration and resentment stemming from their awareness that it is the view of the white man that race differences justify the restrictions which perpetuate the colored peoples' status of inferiority.

Eurasians and Other Mixed Peoples

In the development of nationalist movements, the status of
a Eurasian or of any mixed racial group becomes critical and tragic.
They are neither of the "oppressed" nor are they "the oppressors";
they are identified by nationalists as allied with the whites, yet they
are commonly rejected by the whites. Their problem of accommodation to change is the most acute of all.

It is a problem affecting small groups of peoples in India, Burma,
Indo-China, Indonesia, South Africa, and, indeed, in most areas of
the world where Western man has extended his economic interests
and political control. (The problem is not one related only to Western man or racially mixed peoples. There are equally serious situations in which a distinctive racial minority is sandwiched between
the dominant group and the indigenous peoples: the Chinese in
Malaya, the Indians in Burma and Africa.) A still more complicated situation exists in Sierra Leone, where Creoles, who are
descendants of Africans liberated from slave ships and who came
under extensive missionary influence, are now being excluded from
positions in their society by other Africans, although in many
respects they could perform highly useful services.

One possible exception to the generalization that Eurasians or
other mixed racial groups may not play important roles in nationalist movements is found in the case of the East and South African
Indian. It is an important exception in view of the prominence of
India and her interest in race situations, especially where Asian and
European peoples are involved. If in the past the Indian has been
regarded with disfavor by Africans and Europeans alike, and rel-
egated by the latter to "unassimilable" status, with consequent restrictions on movement, housing, occupation, and political activities,
there are signs that an alliance is evolving between some African
nationalists and Indians. The whites have contributed to, and, in
effect, forced this development by their attitudes and policies. The
Indians are suspected of receiving financial support and advice from
the Congress Party at home and its African branches. Etched in the

memory of Indians is the fact that Gandhi's nonviolence protest movement originated in South Africa. Many of the passive-opposition techniques of African protest movements are based upon his model. The possibility that Indians may yet play an important, if numerically small, part in African nationalism adds a new and vital dimension to African developments.

Integration

Yet, important developments in the relations between native peoples and dominant groups may take the form of acculturation. While this might be expected to occur more frequently in cases where the dominant group is also larger numerically than the indigenous people (as in Australia), the process of acculturation may occur when there is no one group in the population so large as to constitute a particular racial majority (as in Hawaii). Integration may be a very much more complex process than nationalism; symbols of racial unity and nationalism are obviously not available to those who pursue this goal. The nationalist movement does not depend, in the final sense, on any willingness or reasonableness of the ruling colonial society to accept it, for force remains the ultimate weapon. In integration, however, there must be a significant number of the dominant group willing to engage in the process. Within the interracial movement which develops, a degree of social equality exists unknown outside its confines, and those who participate find themselves not infrequently scorned by rulers and ruled alike. As the post-domination period continues there will be important changes in the attitudes of groups within the communal society; some in the dominant and ruled groups will resent any amelioration of racial attitudes; both sides regard it as appeasement. The outspoken proponent of political freedom and social equality will be damned as well as the conservative advocate of the status quo. But reactions are complicated and become modified with time. One cannot categorize the rulers or the ruled as representing a fixed, unchanging view of only one part of the racial spectrum. A study of trends in race relations might be made of the views within communal groups as nationalism or integration or absorption become forces making for change.

Several conference members said that the usefulness of dividing the history of contact between peoples into these four phases of pre-contact, contact, domination, and post-domination depends on the extent to which none of these categories is regarded as a strait-jacket. For, in all periods, key individuals are found who are either in advance of their time or who lag behind. These persons who initiate change or keep the status quo are among the most important subjects for study in evolving race situations. A French member described to the conference a variation of the historical approach: the period of "active acceptance," followed by a period of limited co-operation with the dominant minority, then "passive acceptance"— no element of resistance to sudden economic and political change, "passive opposition," which may take the form of "nonviolence" resistance movements of the Gandhi pattern, counter-racism, or perhaps a renaissance of interest in one's past. Finally, there is "active opposition" which challenges openly the fact of foreign domination.

The South Pacific and Race Situations

A member familiar with race issues in the South Pacific offered still another set of terms which he had found useful in his studies of the Australian aborigines, the Melanesians, and the Polynesians.

He suggested that the reactions of these people can be studied under three phases of racial contact, the first being characterized largely by ambivalence where "fear, bewilderment, curiosity, and hostility" are all expressed. The attitudes adopted by each depend partly on the attitudes and behavior of the newcomer and partly on the attitudes of the native peoples "to the outsider and the unknown." The initial reaction is followed, if permanent settlement by the newcomer takes place, by a period of acceptance and adjustment to the new. The impact of the newcomer's culture, values, and demands is great, and, while there may be groups or individuals who express their reaction by withdrawing from contact, most, in association with the newcomer, tend to become part of his system either as laborers, sources of produce, or as servants. Passive resistance is broken down; there is an attraction for some of the goods of the white man, and to acquire these the native must become involved with the new.

This initial period is followed by one of disillusionment and dissatsifaction for, as we have seen, "working for the white man, buying what he sells, learning to read and write a little, and accepting his religion—these things, acts, and accomplishments, either singly or collectively, do not give entry into the white man's world of possessions, knowledge, or power." In reaction to this, the native may withdraw, disillusioned and at the same time dissatisfied, taking refuge in his own system which has itself been altered. Turning back, he develops new attitudes toward the white man; he may become hostile or non-co-operative, "fantasy-ridden," or "two-faced." This phase is followed by the recovery of solidarity or self-assertion in which the challenge posed by the settlers is accepted and the reconciliation and adjustment occur.

The Australian Aborigine

The reaction to the coming of the Europeans varied from Australia to Melanesia and Polynesia depending upon the particular geographical, social, and political backgrounds of the peoples concerned. The impact of Australian immigrants on the aborigine and his way of life was shattering; the immigrants quickly outnumbered the aborigines and the latter saw the new Australians taking the land, developing settlements, and extending political control throughout habitable Australia. The aborigines were food-gathering, hunting peoples organized into a clan and tribal society. It was necessary for them to accommodate themselves to the new ways or perish. Their accommodation came about partly as a result of the extension of ranch flocks and herds into more arid areas. The aborigine was suited for the labor requirements of the station camps, and, desiring some of the goals of the white Australians, a gradual accommodation was reached between the two groups. Out of this association developed, in time, health and educational measures which prevented the extinction of the aborigines and which have contributed to his new feelings of solidarity and self-assertion.

Those who are of mixed blood have made the most extensive accommodation and have begun to organize themselves and protest developments adversely affecting their position and rights. (These marginal peoples are in contrast to many of the aborigines who continue to live in poverty, lead shiftless lives, and have not begun to make an accommodation.) The initial revival of solidarity of the part-aborigines is manifest, for example, by revival of old customs and pseudo-Christian religious revivals. More recently, with improved welfare and education services, they have come to find for themselves a certain place in the community.

Generally speaking, however, the form which this revival of solidarity has taken should be described in social rather than political terms, although several movements have taken on the latter significance. Part of the response leading to greater solidarity is a result of the racial attitudes of the white Australian, which have caused the part- and full-blooded aborigines on occasion to band together. This race problem is likely to continue as the aborigines demonstrate their solidarity by further organization among themselves and as the white Australians differentiate even the part-aborigines, who remain isolated, as a special social group because of distinctions in color.

The Maoris

New Zealand is a different story; there, initial contact was between Maoris and a few Europeans. There was none of the sudden and critical flow of immigrants which poured into Australia. The Maoris certainly had a more developed culture and organization, which gave them greater strength vis-a-vis the European and better means to assert their rights than were available to the aborigines. Problems between the Maoris and Europeans became explosive when the nineteenth-century flow of immigrants reached New Zealand in significant number, and competition for land became of critical importance to both groups. The disastrous wars of the mid-nineteenth century ended in Maori defeat. Many withdrew from European contact, and general disillusionment and apathy was widespread. Subsequently, some Maoris actively sought ways to accommodate themselves to the new, trying to preserve as much of their background and ways as possible. This process has been made more difficult by the definite race prejudice found on the part of the white New Zealander, who exhibits something of the same color attitude as the white Australian. This means that, for the Maori and the aborigine, solidarity is expressed through their own societies and beliefs, the development of an awareness of their separateness, and a realization that they face the problem of color in any effort made to break from their group to seek full assimilation into the world of whites. (There is an interesting parallel here between these views and those advanced by South Africans to justify Apartheid.) For the future, these "communal" societies will develop along lines which will serve to make them even more distinctive. In the absence of any indication that color consciousness will disappear from the minds of the great majority of white Australians and New Zealanders, the future of the aborigines and Maoris would seem to lie in their separate groups and an increased sense of solidarity expressed through these associations. Underlying many of these movements is the belief that their survival as a people depends upon that solidarity, and their unity finds expression in a concept of race.

New Guinea and Polynesia

In both New Zealand and Australia, the indigenous peoples were displaced by the Europeans who became the dominant economic and political group. This displacement of indigenous peoples did not occur in other island areas such as New Guinea and throughout

most of Polynesia (Hawaii excepted). There has been no critical
alienation of land from the Melanesians, partly due to difficult living
conditions and partly due to preventive measures taken by the
colonial administrations. Where Maori reaction became eventually
one of war for their independence and the response of the aborigine
finally one of seeking accommodation to the European, the peoples
of New Guinea have expressed their reaction "by way of myth and
magico-religious ritual." Race problems among these peoples arose
out of labor and ignorance about the source of the European wealth.

Still another form of response occurred in areas of Polynesia
where the indigenous peoples did not as a whole find their ways of
life and customs abruptly ended. The other Polynesians have not
been faced with the possibility feared by Maoris and aborigines that,
as indigenous people, they would eventually be lost into the larger,
growing, immigrant population. Furthermore, they have frequently
had colonial administrations which have given them a measure of
protection. With strong leadership they have accepted some aspects
of European ways and rejected others. They have sought a satisfying
measure of assimilation within self-defined limits. In this process
a "phase of stabilization" has been reached in the course of which
these Polynesians (notably the Samoans and Tongans) did not experience a loss of solidarity and did not become remnant groups of
peoples splintered by European immigration and the impact of European ideas.

Whether one considers the Maori or the Australian aborigine, the
New Guinea peoples or the Samoans, one appreciates the difficulties
of those who are neither fully part of the old traditional ways nor
part of the new. These "marginal people" are often the ones who
sense their inadequacy most and who become conscious first of the
factor of race in their adjustment.

Native peoples are confronted with an immense problem when we per-
suade or oblige them to readapt themselves quickly to our introduced economic, political, moral, and religious customs, institutions, and requirements.
On the one hand, none of these has any historical-adaptational significance

for them; and on the other hand, their significance for us, the culture-bearers, is only incidentally concerned with Melanesia or New Guinea. It lies in our home country and in Western civilization. Melanesians and Papuans knowing nothing of this, are hard put to find a satisfying meaning in what we require them to do and to be. They must, however, adapt themselves to the new factors in the environment, namely, the planter, miner, missionary, and official. The "must," however, is softened by the new desire for certain introduced goods and, in time, for medical treatment and education.

Outwardly, the natives may seem satisfied and even adjusted, but we know little of their thoughts and private lives. Circumstances eventually arise, however, in which another side is revealed. The recent war in New Guinea was such a circumstance. For example, natives in the Markham Valley, who had apparently been loyal Lutherans for a generation and more, began performing indigenous magico-religious ritual. When questioned about this seeming revival, they replied that they had never ceased to perform the ritual, for otherwise they could not have been assured of their crops and of their own well-being. They had been good Lutherans during the day, but good pagans in the secrecy of the night and the bush.

Reference was made during the conference to a number of examples of this "double life." One which aroused considerable interest, and was included in the conference paper on the South Pacific and Australia, concerned the so-called Cargo Cults. Since little is known about these cults and since they represent a particular kind of reaction to European man, extended remarks about them seem appropriate.

The Cargo Cults

Conference members with African experience drew attention to the striking parallels between these Cargo Cults and African nativistic religious movements (reviewed in Chapter 6). The Pacific and African movements have a common origin. At one and the same time they are expressions of revolt against the changes wrought by Western man, of frustration of the indigenous peoples over their inability to lead their own lives uninterruptedly, and yet are reflective of a desire to emulate the West and obtain its goods. In both the African and Pacific examples there is embodied in their ritual and beliefs a crude attempt to imitate some Western ideas and practices. While both may be described as embryonic nationalist movements, the Cargo Cult is described here to illustrate the contradictory reactions and responses of an indigenous people to an outside, dominant group.

The Cargo Cults are found in many scattered areas of the Southwest Pacific and have a number of features in common. They have their origin in the anticipated arrival of a ship or aircraft whose cargo includes European items which they have learned to need or to desire. The natives react to the impending arrival in what was described as either a positive or negative fashion. If the former, the natives

may "perform ritual acts, pray, 'shake,' and go into trances; shift or leave their villages, sometimes construct and live in communal houses; build storehouses to hold the good things to come, and even store symbolic objects in these to be changed by spiritual agency into desired material objects; erect flagpoles and wireless masts; observe certain codes of behavior, in some cases pagan, in some Christian; and drill, frequently with dummy rifles." If the negative reaction occurs, they may "cease normal food production, kill their pigs, and consume all their garden produce; throw away or spend all their European money; withdraw from contact with Europeans and live an independent, self-ordered mode of existence. The withdrawal may also include an element of hostility. Thus, a catastrophe of nature may be expected which will overwhelm those who do not join the movement, and also the whites; and in some cases the spirits and the cargo (especially of rifles) will enable the followers of the cult to kill or drive the Europeans away. (No one outbreak necessarily includes all these positive and negative actions.)

The positive reaction is based on a belief, itself based on indigenous doctrine, that the goods expected will be brought to them by spirits of the dead—that they are the active agents, called as a result of ritual, and are the ones responsible for the arrival. In the leadership of the cult, "one man (a female in two cases) is the prophet of God or of some specially named spirit, or is the medium through which the spirits of the ancestors or the gods make demands and promises known. He usually possesses uncontested authority and, in some cases, distinct organizing power. He may have held a position of minor authority under Europeans, such as *luluai,* police sergeant, boss-boy, or lay missionary."

If the cargo fails to arrive, the movement collapses. Although the natives return to their normal life, it is certain that "a strong conviction emerges that their well-being lies in their own self-determined social, moral, and ritual order, into which they must bring whatever they desire and can of European culture, the secret of which, however, evades them." The ambivalence of these cults— the sense of fear and expectancy, and the acceptance of the trader as one of their own spirits—is evident in the ritual. Efforts to nip the movements in the bud by arrests and courts only make them quiescent, for these measures are interpreted as showing that the Europeans believe in the efficacy of the Cults to cause cargoes to materialize, but that they are determined not to let them fall into the natives' hands. So faith is strengthened.

Administrations in earlier decades were apt to regard the outbreaks as fantasy expressions of primitive reaction to change, which would lose their potency of their own accord. The spread of the Cults and definite anti-white aspects resulted in firmer and repressive action, which, however, is only a temporary measure. Therefore, resort is being made to educating the natives about the processes and work involved in producing "cargo." Visits to Australia have been arranged, but this has not proved as effective as hoped. To them something besides work seems involved: a secret which the white man keeps to himself. They saw white, black, and yellow men working hard during the war years, but that work did not produce goods. Indeed, more and greater miraculous cargoes arrived—too much to be made by work.

That, however, is not the fundamental issue. The leader, the spirits of the ancestors, the cargoes, the self-organization and discipline, the amalgam of indigenous and introduced (religious and military) elements in the ritual, the withdrawal from active participation in European activity, are all symbolic of that issue: (1) disillusionment and dissatisfaction with native-European relations, economic, political, and religious; (2) resentment at the constant interference in the self-regulation of life; and (3) a "return to the mat": that is, a return to the old faith and ritual, though modified by mission influences; to non-European activities, though desiring European goods; and to self-organization and self-government, though somehow within the European setup.

This program of "return," of weaving selected new strands into the old mat, has proved, as yet, beyond the powers of Melanesians and Papuans, but the very attempts and failures check the tendency to rush, or to be rushed forward too fast, and to become counterfeit Europeans. They also serve to build up concepts of ever-widening solidarity. The more sophisticated use such phrases as "we New Guinea people." Therefore, we cannot but recognize a political and nascent national aspect to these cults. Indeed, this is the significant thing about them, not the resort to fantasy realization. The so-called fantasy springs from the doctrine and ritual of their own culture. It is continuity being reaffirmed, and hope engendered.

The political aspect was, of course, very obvious in the Masinga movement of the British Solomons, and has been patent at times in the history of contact in the Madang region and in Manus. But it is seldom absent. Moreover, where there is no such cult, there may still be much questioning and criticism of features of the contact position. In 1946, members of the Papuan Infantry Battalion made it quite clear to me that they wanted a better deal than they had received in prewar days: they wanted better education (they wanted their girls taught home- and mother-craft, not just to wash the floors of missionaries' houses); they wanted co-operative plantations in which each could contribute according to his skill. In Manus, the demand was for English, not pidgin, and to be left alone to reorganize their own villages and gardens after the upset of the war. They added quite frankly that while they would send small teams to assist the administrative officer, they would not work for the planter—not yet, at any rate. They had too much reconstruction to do.

A stage arises in the course of contact when Papuans and Melanesians consider that they are not receiving all they should in return for their labor, for the white man's presence in, and use of, their country, or for his ordering of their lives and thought. As a reaction, without wanting to go back to the old times, they do want, once again, to run their own lives, and to progress in their own way by getting education from the European and also the "secret" of his goods, his cargo. To them, race relations present the problem of self-determination, and self-satisfaction, and they are showing in cult movements, as well as in direct approaches, that they can think on these things.

Chapter 5

NEW PEOPLES AND NEW ELITES

Sources utilized in this chapter include, in addition to the conference reports and discussions, the following papers in Andrew W. Lind, ed., Race Relations in World Perspective *(Honolulu: University of Hawaii Press, 1955): "New Peoples," by Everett Hughes; "The Negro in the United States," by E. Franklin Frazier; "Adjustment Problems of Negro and Immigrant Elites," by T. S. Simey; and "The African Elite in British West Africa," by Kenneth Little.*

New Peoples

After discussing the response of certain indigenous peoples to Western expansion, the conference members focused their attention on a phenomenon of continuing importance in Eurasia and Africa: the emergence of what has been called "new peoples" and "new elites."

"New people" is a term applied to a group whose antecedents lie deep in history but who have gained a new sense of unity and purpose which distinguishes them from that past. In one conference paper, the example of the Jews was cited as an old people, the Israeli today being one of the new. The people of India have a great past, but, in the sense they are acquiring a new unity and purpose within the modern Indian state and gaining new conceptions of themselves, they would be considered a new people. Americans today are certainly a new people, when one considers the disparate national and racial backgrounds from which the immigrants came and the sense of unity and purpose distinguishing them from their past. The peoples of British West Africa, themselves old, are in their evolution becoming a new people. Nowhere is this process complete,

95

but out of events of the nineteenth and twentieth centuries there are now taking place striking changes in the way in which many peoples have associated themselves together. Today there are new unities with distinctive purposes and objectives.

These new peoples may have, as in the case of the Israeli, a presumed common racial origin, but they may also represent diverse cultural patterns. The European Jews and the Jews of Yemen are, for all practical purposes, two peoples attempting to unite. There are similar differences in other new peoples, which suggest that in the gaining of this new unity and consciousness, a key process is that of extensive cultural change. In the case of Hawaii, where one sees a half-dozen peoples of varying national and racial origins becoming interracial, one is struck by the fact that this change is contemporaneous with the adaptation of their own particular cultural backgrounds to the American background. Consequently a new sense of identification, a sense of sharing in a common purpose is emerging, which increasingly frees itself from its old racial or national setting.

The conference was told at length about the cultural transformations occurring in parts of West Africa. Unlike Hawaii, British West Africa has no significant number of permanent white settlers, and the process of becoming a new people is not one of an interracial character but one of cultural adaptation and assimilation on the part of the native Africans. Similarly, in Central Asia the modern consciousness of the Moslems implies a cultural reorientation only and does not involve a racial mixture with European Russians. As in all other aspects of race relations, the situations are varied, complex, and dynamic.

The role of imperial powers has been important in encouraging the emergence of "new peoples" if the controlling group is tolerant of miscegenation, supports cultural assimilation through schools and advanced training of indigenous leaders, and permits indigenous organizations of a political, cultural, social, or economic character to function.

The revival of a sense of new unity was encouraged indirectly in a number of colonial areas, especially in southern Asia and in Southeast Asia, by the governing and administrative policies of the British. These policies, implemented at the end of the nineteenth century for parts of Africa and, somewhat later, for the Indian subcontinent and Burma, were partly the expression of an often-stated belief in the tutelary role of Great Britain, ending "in due course" in independence. They were adopted also because the British believed that native institutions and hierarchy could be used to implement British policy and further British interests and yet preserve something of the indigenous culture and beliefs from the disintegrating effect of the sudden impact of Western man and his ways.

Conference members were told how extensive the influence of Communist ideology and tactics has been in the encouragement of a new sense of unity and purpose among colonial peoples. Soviet influence has been important in feeding the fires of a new consciousness, usually expressed in political nationalism and usually including in some degree an element of race consciousness.

The United States has also played an important though different role. American insistence on the right of self-determination gave great encouragement to ethnic groups during and after World War I. While national revivals were already occurring in colonial areas of Asia and among some of the North African and European peoples, the ideological impact of the principle of self-determination resulted in political action having as its objective freedom within new states based largely on ethnic or presumed ethnic bases.

In several instances today, free people are becoming "new" as a result of direct government action. In such cases, the state consciously seeks to integrate more closely its peoples of diverse backgrounds, thereby creating a new sense of unity and purpose. Israel is a key example and Burma is another, with the government of the Union trying in its administration and policies to fashion a unified modern state. In Burma, Israel, and many other nations, stress is laid upon the encouragement and training of a more adequate leadership, which breaks with the past and becomes an important innovator in all fields of society. Several states seek also to revive and sometimes "modernize" traditional unifying factors, such as religion, to meet the needs of the new society. Burma is trying this with an intensive effort to revive interest in Buddhism, and in Indonesia and Pakistan a similar activity is under way with respect to Islam.

Acute problems of adjustment occur in any effort by a people to adopt new values, customs, and institutions. The quality of leadership available to them is obviously of great importance. The several examples briefly noted here show the efforts of a whole people or a majority of those in an area to transform much of their lives. There are other instances of adaptation which concern the efforts of minority groups seeking assimilation into the life of the community which surrounds them. Insofar as their efforts meet with success, such groups are also to be considered as "new peoples." Reports of Negro adjustment in the United States and Great Britain were discussed as case examples of such efforts.

The American Negro. The American Negro was discussed in the light of his relative isolation from the main stream of American life during much of his history in the New World, an experience unlike that of most European immigrants, who became fully assimilated. Aspects of Negro adjustment were discussed also in the context of changing patterns of race relations. A basic feature differentiating the American Negro's adjustment from that of European immigrant groups to the United States, and distinguishing it from the experiences of indigenous peoples of Africa and Asia is the fact that the Negro's traditional, social, and cultural bonds were severed by slavery—his separation from his tribal and kinship group was complete and abrupt. As a consequence, the Negro, cut off from the familiar, had to adjust to the new without the benefit of a gradual transition from the old. In the process, he developed new concepts of himself and new outlooks on life. Christianity played a key part in his new orientation.

In his adjustment there appears to have been no important movement of any lasting consequence which sought to revive or develop
among and for American Negroes a special Negro culture or way
of life. The emphasis has been on Negro assimilation into American ways. The majority of plantation Negroes became "accommodated to an inferior position in the white man's world, thought
of themselves as inferior, and could hope for no higher status." But
there were always Negroes "who, because they had caught glimpses
of a wider world, dreamed of freedom, if not equality, in the white
man's world." Negroes who had been given freedom, who had fled
slavery, or had worked at jobs outside the plantation system gained
still another conception of themselves and their fellow men. In the
post-Civil War era there was great bewilderment among the freed-
men; their pattern of life did not conform fully with American ways.
The Negro family lacked the cohesiveness of the American family;
Negro children were not molded in any family or cultural tradition
except that of "a simple folk tradition in which the Christian religion was the most important element. After the political struggles
and vicissitudes of the Reconstruction Period, which ended in disillusionment concerning the meaning of freedom, the masses of
Negroes resigned themselves to their inferior status in a white man's
world and only hoped to escape from their inferiority after death."

The rapid urbanization of the postwar period brought increasing
numbers of Negroes into contact with a new world, and as a result,
Negroes began to lose their "other-worldly" outlook and to gain a
more secular view. One Negro movement of some importance was
the Garvey movement. It captured the imagination of "the disillusioned black masses [who] sought to escape from the frustrations
and contempt of the white man's world. Africa became for the first
time a promised land for a large number among the Negro masses."
The movement was short-lived, and Negroes began to join labor
unions and other groups connected with urban life and the accelerating pace of industrialization.

The new orientation of the educated Negro toward his position in American life found expression in the Negro Renaissance, in which Negro writers, poets, and painters undertook to reinterpret and re-evaluate the history and experiences of the Negro. It was the hope of the leaders of the Negro Renaissance that through a re-evaluation of the Negro's experience in American life the Negro would acquire a new conception of himself. But the Negro Renaissance appealed principally to the Negro intelligentsia. It failed to gain the support of the increasing number of middle-class Negroes who only desired to mold themselves in the image of the whites. A French sociologist who visited the United States was struck by the "black Babbitts" in northern cities.

.   .   .   .

Not being rooted in a cultural heritage, the personality of the Negro has revealed a certain emptiness, especially since the Negro has not found acceptance in American society and he has not been able to identify completely with Americans.

It is difficult to say what direction the development of his personality will take as he becomes increasingly integrated into American life. Some may lose completely their identification as Negroes; while at the same time, with the increasing importance of Africans in the modern world, some may seek a new identification with the Africans.

The Negro in Great Britain. The Negro in Great Britain is another example of attempted adjustment. The Negroes are almost all immigrant laborers from Africa or the West Indies, or are in Britain as students for short periods of time. There is a general British belief that the Negro background and culture are inferior, and this belief is shared by many of the Negroes themselves. Among immigrants, the acknowledgement of this inferiority is evident by the very act of migration and the subsequent effort to become part of British society. As the Negro attempts to enter the margins of British society he becomes adrift, losing many of his familiar contacts and supports in the effort to become part of the new. This is an effort not always sympathetically accepted in the British, with the inevitable result that the Negro becomes "rootless," no longer fully accepted in the old and by no means at home in the new.

Variations in the attitude toward British society appear among West Indians, African Negroes, and Asians. Those who have a background in a recognized culture do not feel the pressures experienced by West Indians and Africans, who are more likely to be overtly hostile and more "inclined to interpret everything from an exclusively racial and nationalist angle." Students from the West Indies are halfway between the Asian and Africans in this respect. A few with outstanding educational records or unusual ability may be able to become assimilated in British society, while many more find some measure of partial personal accommodation to that society. Student societies play an important part in this process; the West African Students' Union has been regarded as a training ground of political experience, and a number of leading Africans have gained early and useful experience in the Union. But the organization also serves a useful purpose for the African in that it is a channel or outlet for the resentment (not unmixed with a personal sense of humiliation) experienced by the African in his life in the imperial country where the existence of a color bar is apparent. The organization may also be regarded as serving a further purpose in that it gives the members "a new consciousness of their own value and capacity for achievement." The isolating effect such organizations have on African students makes their assimilation more difficult. However, since the student expects to return to his African area, their isolation is not as important a factor as it would be if he were of the working class colonial immigrant type who seeks to reduce the contacts he has among people of his background in order to become part of British society as rapidly and as completely as possible. Those who lack the initiative or the opportunity to succeed in this course will generally revert to a lower level and, usually in a dockland or similar depressed area, discover some small familiar society of their own.

Among Negro groups there are two distinct pulls: one seeks to draw the Negro out of his group into closer association with British, and the other is that magnetism which not unexpectably attracts him to organizations composed of his own people. If these organizations have any influence, they will make possible a greater degree of solidarity and will reduce thereby the opportunity for an African to depart from his group into a closer association with the British. "The fact is that the African group is pulling against itself. There is a counter process operating toward dissolving the colored group and integrating its members with the white society."[1]

For the West Indian immigrant another divisive factor stems from his individualism and competitive spirit. Class and status count in his society, where successful immigrants are regarded jealously by the others. Those who succeed generally leave their society and seek a closer association with the British. Those who do not succeed are usually poorly adjusted and generally of inferior ability. There is a deep gulf between them and British society, and between them and their more successful friends. The Negroes who remain within the group include a relatively large number of those who will be likely to earn their fellows a "bad name."

Here again, the Asians in England appear to be under less strain, since they seek adjustment, not assimilation. In their case, traditional sources of leadership give them a sense of continuity and an important sense of cohesiveness. But when an Asian immigrant finds employment outside his group, he comes under many of the same pulls to accomplish some degree of assimilation. These pulls are again prime causes of the breakdown of his solidarity and, as in the situation of the Negro immigrant, the ease of his accommodation will depend significantly on whether the effort is one undertaken by many in his group or by a few who in the process and for a time become distinct, both from their own group and from British society.

Those interested in the problem of encouraging the assimilation of racial groups into a national society suggested that while a number of personal contacts can be made between members of that society and persons of the immigrant group under a variety of circumstances, most effective progress can be made where it is possible

---

[1] S. Collins, "Social Processes Integrating Coloured People in Britain," *The British Journal of Sociology* (1952).

to work through the immigrants' leadership: the modifications inherent in any process of assimilation may be achieved best through
the use of leaders acknowledged to be such by the groups concerned. To be successful, this requires the discovery of those who
can preserve their traditional position in a period of great change.
We know too little today about the requirements of leadership to
effect this transition among the masses, although the discovery of
such leaders may be of vital consequence to national security and
progress.

⌐Our knowledge of the conditions which determine the emergence of new
elites and the survival of the old elites is pitifully weak. ¬We know that the
best adjustments appear to be made in British society by skilled workers, and
that such people comprise an elite rather better educated and more sophisticated than their fellows. But the members of this elite not only tend to
separate themselves from the rest of the colored community by reason of the
types of employment in which they are engaged, but are also distinguished
from the masses by their clothes, their possessions, and their personal habits.
⌐This knowledge applies only to the very special circumstances obtaining in
Great Britain; however, a study of the emergent leader would be much more
illuminating if it could be carried out in the West Indies or in Israel, regions
which are inhabited by communities in which a leader has a much better
chance to establish his position by fighting *for* rather than *against* something.⌐
In sum, the possibilities for the emergence of a leader who is able to con-
solidate his position on a basis of mutual trust and esteem, and lead a people
or a group toward the achievement of new standards and patterns of behavior which his followers will recognize as worth while, are much more
evident where the assimilation of cultures is an ongoing process, which is
plain to everybody. It is poorest in those societies in which the processes of
change are restricted to the adjustment of an inferior to a superior culture.
. . . In the long run, adjustment will be a successful process, and leaders
will come forward to carry it out, only if assimilation is a possible alterna-
tive to adjustment.⌐ No leader is likely in the twentieth century to survive
the perils and the pains of leading his people to a position of permanent inferiority or subjection; which leads one to conclude that the social patterns
which will be characteristic of the new world to come will be shaped, in the
first instance, in such countries as Israel and the West Indian territories.⌐

In discussing "new peoples" then, the conference was reviewing
a situation found in many areas scattered around the world. The
emphasis, again, is on change, and the critical factor is the nature

and quality of the leadership which is emerging. In certain cases, the leaders may have a background of a developed culture and be familiar with the mechanisms of modern government. In other cases, the leaders themselves may be passing through a period of transition, as in the case of Oriental Jewry in Israel, or in the case of tribal chiefs in parts of Africa. In most instances there is a close relationship between the leaders of the elites and the process of cultural assimilation or synthesis under way.

New Elites

British West Africa. In considering the many facets of adaptation or assimilation and the emergence of new leadership, the presence in the conference of a number of Europeans and Africans of special familiarity with developments in certain areas of that continent meant that sessions were of the most interest when focused on Africa. Discussions at the various round tables were based on a series of papers prepared on the subject of cultural adaptation and elites in Southern and British West Africa. Discussion centered first on British West Africa.

The process of "Westernization" began some three hundred years ago when the first Europeans established trading posts and forts. In the Gold Coast, labor and trade requirements created small communities of Africans located near these centers. The obvious need for translators and go-betweens meant some Western education was desirable, and the English established schools. They also introduced Christianity. Some Africans were sent to England.

Throughout the last century the British expanded their control beyond the trading centers, and, largely for commercial reasons, finally assumed political power over all of what is now the British Gold Coast. The small African communities connected with these centers produced a small group of educated Africans, who have emerged as a new African elite. In another area, farther west, the unique development of Sierra Leone has given rise to a very much larger African elite with a far greater impact of European ideas throughout the area than is the case in the Gold Coast or Nigeria.

Sierra Leone, originally conceived of as a home for indigent Negroes from England, became a naval base in the nineteenth century in the British effort against the slave trade. Captured slaves were freed and given land. The British also regarded Sierra Leone as the base of civilizing and Christianizing operations into the African interior. A rigorous system of indoctrination and compulsory child education was instituted. As a result of these intensive efforts, much of their tribal past became forgotten, and a unique group of Africans emerged whose descendants have as part of their own background a significant degree of Westernization. While there were many opportunities in mission work, government service, and business for the people of Sierra Leone, their greatest contribution to the Westernization of British West Africa came in their spread out of the area of Sierra Leone proper into the Gold Coast and Nigeria and, in fact, along the entire West African coast. While these people were limited to areas under some degree of British control, they managed in time to exert considerable influence over people and chiefs of the interior.

Final steps in the extension of British control were taken in the later years of the nineteenth century and in the period following World War I. These steps transformed the relationship between British and Africans. The British limited tribal authority, ended the native wars, and extended commercial posts throughout the interior. For the first time the British established general political and administrative control. During all this, Africans played an important role in the British administration. A number of them were attracted to colonial service because of social prestige, the new freedoms from tribal life, and the desirability of Western goods.

While employment by the British resulted in a loss of tribal connections, this loss had to be evaluated along with one's association with the ruler and a growing familiarity with his standards and customs.

Those Africans who became members of the professional class, doctors and lawyers in particular, were regarded with respect by British and Africans alike, giving them special opportunities to transmit Western ideas. Educational and health services, the economic demands for colonial products, and various schemes such as the Colonial Development and Welfare acts facilitated this process. Africans who sought opportunities in the new towns kept, for a time at least, their tribal identity. Eventually these tribal ties were loosened and the urban worker identified himself increasingly with Western-style societies and organizations. In short, British efforts in Sierra Leone and the Gold Coast have been such as to make possible the growth of this relatively small but increasingly important segment of the African population which plays a key role, not just as low- or middle-level colonial servants, but as a respected group which has now become a modern African elite.

The peoples of the Gold Coast, then, who only a few decades ago were illiterate, tribally divided, and had a subsistence economy, are now on the threshold of political freedom and national independence. The transition has been extensive and rapid and is a graphic example of the emergence of a "new people." In this period of striking change, the emphasis has been on African "adaptation to the ideas, methods, and material equipment imported from the West rather than an adjustment to Europeans as a human group." The problem of relationships between the West African and the British has been one of cultural adaptation by the African and not one in which any issue of race figured importantly. The major task has been and remains one of "reconciling what traditionally exists with what is deemed necessary for the sake of political, economic, and social development."

The rapidity of political and cultural change is impressive but is by no means experienced in equal degree throughout all areas of West Africa. There are great differences among Africans in levels of education, in culture and language, and an infinite number of gradations from the "bush African" of no contact with any world other than his tribal one to the educated professional African, educated at Oxford or Cambridge with ministerial rank. Because of the differences in experience and learning and because of the British policy of eventual independence, the key relationship is not that between the British and African elites but between the modern African elite and the greater number of his people who are still tribally bound and largely lacking in modern education.

The Challenge to African Elites. Black African social divisions reflect the varying impact of the West. There are those on whom the impact has been greatest and who have gone the farthest in Westernization. They constitute the educated class, the critical African elite. Next in order come the semiliterate or those who have had less contact and perhaps fewer opportunities to develop away from the tribal past. Finally, there are those who remain most closely linked to traditional Africa and who have been relatively isolated from European contact. The challenge to the African elite is one of leading a nation so socio-culturally divided. In so classifying divisions of African society, a European measuring stick is basic. For the present, the African elite must be examined against that measure. Europeans are not, of course, part of the African society, but they have an important position because of the symbolic importance attached to their customs and material goods. Their way of life remains a pattern copied as much as possible. Little is known by the indigenous peoples of the personal ideas of the European. However, their customs, manner of dress, recreational activities, clubs, architecture, and conveniences are observed and imitated whenever possible. Notice is also taken of the social hierarchy of the Europeans.

The political and administrative service is paramount and is followed, in approximate order, by those "in the legal and medical branches, police, education, agriculture," etc. This pattern is duplicated largely by the small group of African elites who are the "doctors, administrative officers, secretaries to ministers in the government, university lecturers, nursing sisters, headmasters," etc. Doctors and lawyers rank high, as do educated chiefs and tribal rulers. The new indigenous elite group will have its clerks, community groups, sports, and the mannerisms and dress of their European counterparts.

The semiliterates are far below the elite in the Westernization process. They have had little schooling but are not always poverty-stricken; some have become successful businessmen and traders. The majority will have semiskilled occupations, be the police, the carpenters, drivers, etc. Their homes will be of poorer quality, the furniture and decorations sparse. The nonliterates form the great bulk of the West African people. They are predominantly concerned with agriculture; they may live in towns and will have a few utensils, clothes, etc., patterned after European design or imported. Much more so than the semiliterates, their social world is found in its traditional, exclusive tribal setting, although there may be new societies or organizations as well. They hold largely to traditional magico-religious beliefs.

The line between nonliterate and educated Africans is an important one. Differences are symbolized in clothing, housing, mannerisms, and organizations which reflect the educated African's higher economic status and greater familiarity with the West. But there are political differences as well. The educated African looks to a Western-style government, which clashes inevitably with customary tribal rules. The British have sought to keep some semblance of hereditary rule but the tendency is strong in the direction of elective, parliamentary rule. Nonliterate African chiefs cannot be expected to deal adequately with matters of complex government policy and finance when their terms of reference are out of a tribal background. The trend toward more democratic rule challenges their authority, thus further dividing one group of Africans from another. The extension of literacy is another continuing and growing threat to traditional authority; greater economic freedom on the part of individuals not only means less dependence on the close tribal relationships but greater social freedom for men and women as well. The greatest current source of tension "is the discrepancy between traditional ideas of proper conduct and behavior and ideas based on Christian and scientific beliefs." Children at school do not learn of the old magico-religious beliefs but of a new world. Parental authority and practices are questioned and family relationships loosened; marriage becomes more of a personal affair on the Western model. This disintegrative process is the basic challenge posed non-literate Africans by the educated, Westernized Africans.

Between the nonliterate and the educated African is the African whose job is of a low level and who moves freely between the traditional African camp and the Westernized one. His job as clerk or teacher is in the latter but his social life and family relationships remain in the former. He is a "cultural hybrid" in that

he is called upon to move in two social worlds, involving quite different norms of conduct and behavior. The kind of behavior expected of him varies with the nature of the situation, and the situation itself is mainly defined by the extent to which Western agencies—in the shape of actual persons such as Europeans or highly Westernized Africans or in the shape of institutions such as an office or a school—are involved. In such cases— at work or at church—he behaves, broadly speaking, as a European would in similar circumstances. In his own home, on the other hand, his actions are largely, though by no means wholly, traditional. This is another way of saying, though at the cost of considerable simplification, that in his private life he is an African; in public, a European.

If the effect of Western rule has been to fragment much of tradi-tional West African society, the adaptation of Africans has resulted in part in the development of a host of organizations and societies; specialization occurs not only in economic life but in all the principal activities of community life. Tribal improvement unions, literary unions, and teachers' unions combine politics with mutual aid, occupational associations, burial and benefit societies. Younger Africans with some Western education are responsible, in large part, for the widespread growth of such groups throughout towns and villages of West Africa. Insofar as the leaders in the unions and societies may and do settle arguments between members, these organizations pose still more challenges to the traditional roles of tribal leaders; their authority is being transferred to these new groups and new leaders at the same time it is being lost in political circles to the educated African.

It is mainly in terms of the interaction of educated Africans and traditional society that African adaptation to Western ideas, methods, and materials has primarily to be viewed. The political, economic, and social activities of this group serve as a bridge between the old and the new orders of life, and are thus also the principal means by which the West African problems of reconciliation are being solved.

Central Africa. Leadership problems in Central Africa—the Rhodesias and Nyasaland—were reviewed in conference sessions as a prelude to the discussions on ideological movements and the extent to which new leadership and thinking have developed a racist content of significance to all of Africa.

British control over the Central Africa area began in the closing years of the nineteenth century. Africans at that time were organized primarily into small chiefdoms. British colonial policy sought to preserve as much of the native society as possible, and toward that end established white district officers to maintain peace and collect taxes, assisted by Africans of authority in the traditional order of society. With the important exceptions of kingdoms in Barotseland and Matabeleland, tribal hierarchic authority was neither as highly developed as in West Africa nor as absent as in the Kenya egalitarian societies. In the Rhodesias and Nyasaland, African chiefs could be more easily manipulated. The British saw in these areas a major source of migrant labor supply for mines in the Union to the south and in British Central Africa itself; they were not interested in the establishment of a permanent, urban-located labor force.

Though the British policy was conservative and objectives limited, the impact of European representatives, customs, and values became important, although not as rapidly nor as extensively as was the case in possessions on the West Africa coast. The cessation of tribal wars, the alienation of some land, the missionaries, and the migrant labor system heralded change. As elsewhere, Africans engaged in new enterprises and in government administrative posts, teachers, and others moved partially or entirely out of the tribal community, thereby challenging traditional leadership. British consolidation of some African groups and refusal to extend recognition to all chiefs led to a group of displaced chiefs and headmen. Those who were recognized may have had more or less authority than before, but it was clear to all concerned that ultimate power now lay in the British administration and no longer with traditional African leadership. In this situation, those Africans who formed the "black screen" between white administration and tribal groups—the clerks and the messengers—became marginal men knowing something of the white man's world and methods and no longer fully part of the traditional tribal system. To these factors which undermined the authority of traditional chiefs was added the proletarian leadership which began emerging in migrant labor ranks.

Today, there are two general leadership groups labeled "indigenous": that of the traditional order partially preserved by British policy, and the *de facto* leaders whose power is based upon new sources unrelated to an African past. (Some leaders in the traditional group have extended their influence to new situations. They may have tribal representatives to maintain contact between urban dwellers and the rural center and they may visit the urban areas personally. Others retain control only over old associations and are becoming less influential.)

In Central Africa there has not been in British policy the ultimate objective of African independence, and therein lie some of the most crucial issues in white-black relationships. White settlers, in contrast to those of West Africa, have shown their intention to keep for themselves political control of the area; the balance of political power has shifted in favor of them at the expense of Whitehall. Africans have become increasingly conscious of the precariousness of their position in urban centers. While living and working in the towns, Africans need strong links to their tribal groups. The tribes require, in turn, possession of land; without it they lose their power and cohesiveness. Alienation of land is the most effective way to accomplish detribalization, and some Africans have feared that federation of British Central Africa, with continuing white control, would result in their loss of land. Africans are also fully conscious of the fact that in the recent political struggles that accompanied this federation, a number of their chiefs were arrested and deposed by British authorities. The continuing importance of some of these chiefs rests in their ability to maintain the crucial rural land holdings. The power of the British to make and unmake these leaders adds, therefore, to the African sense of insecurity. The extent to which African interests can be represented effectively by chiefs elected or appointed by the whites was questioned, and it was obvious to conference members that there was a sharp division of opinion on this point between an African conference member and an Englishman. The African expressed the view that the British-appointed chiefs were not considered by Africans to be appointed always in their interests but usually reflected British interests. This leadership could not, therefore, be described as "indigenous"; leaders should be described as "intercessors" between the whites and Africans. With respect to any crossing of race lines in this all-important matter of leadership, both the British and African members agreed that leadership remained color-bound in contrast to developments in British West Africa.

Chapter 6

RACE AND NATIONALISM

*Sources utilized in this chapter include, in addition to the conference
reports and discussions, the following paper in Andrew W. Lind,
ed.,* Race Relations in World Perspective *(Honolulu: University of
Hawaii Press, 1955): "Expressions of Race Relationships in West
and Central Africa," by Georges Balandier.*

Ideas of Race

Since race or ideas of race have become important in many
nationalist movements which have derived some of their inspiration
from the West, a British conference member suggested some time
be set aside for a discussion of the growth and movement of ideas.
Ideas of race have been transmitted quickly from area to area. A
general understanding of the way certain ideologies have passed
from one group to another would be useful in analyzing the ideas
of race in a number of scattered situations in the world. Such an
analysis, in the areas of the colonial belt, would have to include
reference to the disintegration of traditional authority and ideas or
customs under the impact of the West.

It is necessary "to study the natural history of an ideology under
the mass conditions of modern society, where earlier organizing
features [a hereditary aristocracy and a priesthood guarding and developing sacred truths] no longer prevail." The British member suggested that such a study might be made of the important concept of
"negritude" developed by a French member and discussed below
"as an example of an idea emerging from a mass of feelings, becoming formed, and being taken over by different groups from those in

113

which it appeared." He asked the question: how do ideas of "nation" or "race" develop; and what are the successive stages in the history of the idea?

The original step, he suggested, is taken by an individual—"the thinker" who "forms a complex of ideas around some unifying principle, which becomes an *idée force* and, as it is taken over by others, is often expressed in a brief formula, word, or phrase, which becomes a pole of attraction for feelings." The "thinker" is often himself a "marginal" man and the examples of Turkish nationalism and Zionism were cited. Subsequently, in a second stage, popular thought may associate a new set of ideas with the term or phrase, differing from those originally advanced by the thinker. The new ideas may then become institutionalized.

A third stage still further modifies or transforms the idea.

As the idea becomes confronted with reality, it again changes. It may become embodied in legal codes, practices, and group identification. Two principles come into play: the "principle of identity" through which people come to believe "this is the most important thing about me. I am linked to other people by this common feature"; and the "principle of separation" through which the idea becomes a distinguishing feature between groups—peoples become strangers to one another.

The idea no longer has unifying power for the whole society and may be used by one group against another. The final stage is "the decline of the idea": it grows old, loses its dynamic force, but never quite dies out. New ideas linked with new problems emerge and attract elements from the old complex.

Similarly, "the idea of *race* has reached a turning point." In years past, ideas of race with implications of superiority were used to justify the retention of power and the methods and policies of control. The idea and its expression divided peoples: it attempted to resolve permanently matters of status and role. With the passing of Western imperial control and the development of new ideas and attitudes within the Western world itself, the idea did not die out. There are situations evolving today in which race attitudes remain important: for example, in French North Africa and in Great Britain with her recent large increase of Negro immigrants. But generally speaking, the early vigor of the idea has passed. While Communists and others will use racism as a tool for their own purposes whenever and wherever possible, it seemed clear to several of the conference members that the old expressions of race are not as dynamic as they once were. Some of the feelings expressed heretofore in racism seek new symbols and some have found them in the "working class," or proletariat. As a further illustration, a conference member reported that some African nationalist movements do not use as their symbols ideas and phrases of Western democracy because of their association with colonial rule; "new groups are seeking new ideological symbols."

Nationalism and Equality

The majority of conference reports and papers on race and nationalism were concerned with the area once known as the "colonial belt" of the world: the lands between Gibraltar and the Pacific and from Cape Town to Cairo. In recent history, the common denominator of these lands has been European domination. It is, therefore, the area which has experienced most directly the varied racial attitudes of the West. If racism as such was never the reason for European expansion, attitudes of racial superiority (and sometimes religious zeal) did serve on more than one occasion to justify and rationalize its widespread control and domination.

In discussing the relationship between race and contemporary nationalist movements, conference members stressed repeatedly the fundamental part played by the West in introducing ideas of race superiority and, through the model of the Western state, linking ethnic unity with nationalism. (The widely publicized "right of self-determination" is a recent example of the coupling of race with nationhood and freedom.) While no one would suggest that ideas of race were unknown in Africa or Asia before the coming of European man, his contribution has been in the spreading of the European view of the racial basis or ethnic unity of the modern state.

Conference members were sometimes reluctant to ascribe racist views to situations with which they were familiar when race issues were not an open, explicitly acknowledged factor. The question inevitably arises whether many of the attitudes prevalent in Asia and Africa today do contain an element of racism which must be acknowledged. Asian interest in the defeat of Russia by Japan at the turn of the century is thought to have reflected a widespread interest in the accomplishment of an Asian people combined with general anti-Westernism. Similarly, the interest shown by many non-Communist Asians in the Chinese Communist fight in Korea has been interpreted by some as a further indication of Asian pride in the fact that a great Western power had been stalled. The slogan of the Japanese in the thirties and forties of "Asia for the Asiatics," the revived interest among some groups in Burma, Indonesia, India, and the Middle East in their cultures and religions have been of more than passing interest to observers who detect in several of their expressions a sense of superiority over other beliefs, cultures, and peoples. Recently, the Prime Minister of Japan was quoted as calling for the "racial independence" of his country. Furthermore, to what extent do calls for "Asian unity" contain a racist element largely focused on whites or the West? Is there a deep-seated but not always acknowledged core of racism in these movements of continuing importance in East-West relations? The unwillingness of many Asians and Africans to acknowledge any racist content to their attitudes and actions may well come from a genuine disbelief in and repugnance toward any such concept; it may also reflect an unwillingness to acknowledge such a feeling when it has been so frequently and unhappily considered an attribute of Western civilization. Insofar as East-West relations in general and Burman-British, Indo-Chinese–French, and Indonesian-Dutch relations occur between peoples who differ obviously in color and outward appearance, one should expect that, for many, a convenient racial polarization of problems is involved.

There can be little question of Communist efforts to raise the specter of racism at every conceivable opportunity: to place Asians on one side and Europeans on another by reminding Asians of the superior attitudes and contempt for Asians and Africans shown by a number of Europeans, or to give extensive publicity to race problems within the free world. Few observers of Asian and African affairs would deny that these Communist seeds have fallen on very fertile ground.

In considering race issues and nationalism one returns inevitably to a consideration of the nature and effect of the racial attitudes of Western man in his relationship with other peoples. We must acknowledge that the racial element of nationalist movements derives its strength and pervasiveness from the "psychological damage" done to a people through the discovery that its members are regarded by another as inferior by nature.

Obviously it is of first importance that a close and continuing study be made of the areas in which ideas of race appear to be developing. The conference discussed the race factor first in terms of relatively advanced nations such as India. Some members suggested that racist views to date have not figured prominently among Asians who have a rich cultural background and history. Race may have been used by them as a unifying symbol or as a tactic in the struggle for independence. Once independence has been achieved, racism fades from whatever importance it may have had. Other members were unwilling to accept this view. To them, the fading out of race as an idea cannot be assumed just because it is no longer evident in slogans, speeches, and riots. Memories of race experiences linger and are important.

However, most agreed that racism as an explosive force should be studied first among peoples who do not have the rich cultural history of many Asians. The Asian may assert his equality by pointing to a developed culture antedating Western civilization. This the African cannot do, and he may find himself forced to rely on racist views of his own as a counter to Western racism.

What evidence is there of developments within Africa or elsewhere of a conscious use of racism in any of its forms?

Two such examples in the New World were discussed very briefly by the conference. In Haiti, *"authentiques (real* blacks) have developed a 'right-wing' mythology attached to the idea of being black. The idea of purging 'white blood' existing in the mulatto elite appears in the literature of this wing, which has both a messianic and extreme racist tone. Under the influence of this mythology, the black-mulatto conflict is taking a racist character." One conference member reported that in South America, since World War I, "an ideology of Indian race has been developed based on concepts of 'blood' and 'soil' and sometimes taking the form of a mystical idea of the Indian 'soul.'"

Two additional examples were discussed: the growth of the idea of "negritude" and the development of prophetic and separatist church movements within Africa.

Negritude, Prophetism, and Separatist Churches. If there is developing in Africa or in Asia a nationalist movement with a marked racial content, it will be of the gravest consequence, particularly to the Western world. An African movement which has color as its unifying symbol might result in the mobilization of millions of people against white European man. It requires little imagination to appreciate the consequences of such a development. Because of the importance of this problem, many conference members considered the sessions which reviewed nationalist movements among the most informative.

The conference included in its membership several African and European authorities on the racial content of important African movements. The descriptive term "negritude" has been applied to several of these developments to suggest an African awareness of race and pride in the distinction of color. The French member quoted in his conference paper the remark of another writer, "And if Europe said to Africa: 'Consequently, there is no longer any difference between you and me than that between black and white,' Africa would acquiesce but would put an especially proud stress on that difference."

Negritude is an "exaltation of African-Negro specificity," a "kind of highly elaborated counter-racism." It is found in the poetry and other writings of a group of French-speaking native authors of the postwar period. It involves a "particularly intense racial awareness," not uncoupled to political activity and demands. It is a term descriptive, also, of an appreciation of a new black unity experienced by its adherents, a consciousness of sharing in a past and in the making of the future; it is a term which reflects the totality and distinctiveness of an "African world" and brings to mind similar developments in other nationalist movements of Asia and the Middle East. Insofar as the movement—largely literary to date—seeks a renaissance based on cultural primitivism, it has been criticized by Marxists who consider it a mystical movement divorced from present-day realities.

Another critic was quoted as "rejecting the idea of an 'African Renaissance' to the extent that such an orientation could tend toward 'advocating a cultural primitivism which would turn Tropical Africa into a kind of reserve for ethnologists and (would in fact end by) disarming Africans in their struggle for liberty and progress.'" The same critic (who was Secretary-General of the former *Rassemblement Democratique Africain*) is also quoted as refuting "any approach which gives a privileged position to the race factor." He writes, "it is odd to note that the same men who, a short time ago, admitted assimilation pure and simple are the ones who, today, make the race factor the essential element of the political, social, and cultural development of the Negro peoples."

These rejections are important for they reflect the divisions apparent in African nationalism between those who seek on the one hand a "radical nationalism whose dynamism is due to counter-racism at the same time as to an appeal to traditional values" and, on the other, those who hold "a progressive attitude, Marxist in character, which places in the center of its argumentation the criticism of the colonial system more than the exaltation of race." The French member noted that these discussions affect only a small number of the intellectual elite, but they deserve to be mentioned for similar discussions have also occurred in Southeast Asian nationalist movements. Numbers are not important at this stage. The intellectual elite is necessarily small, but their influence is far greater than numbers alone would indicate.

The important question asked was whether the racial element expressed in negritude has any parallel in other movements more popularly based. In partial answer, the conference was fortunate to have two other related movements discussed by French and African members: "prophetism" and separatist churches. Both movements are related in that they draw heavily upon the form and to some extent on the content of the Christian faith. They are of particular interest because they represent in many areas the first steps toward a new organization of Africans.

Throughout South and Central Africa and in French Guinea "one observes the appearance of a native church influenced by nationalist claims or the development of dissident churches giving expression to undeniable race feelings." These movements have several non-religious aspects which give them a special importance. First, they are permanent, not transitory; they seek a new basis of an African social organization and African unification in place of the traditional fragmentation of Africans into tribe and clan. Second, they have grown significantly during periods of serious crisis in relationships between Negroes and whites. The period following World War I with the depressed colonial markets, the great depression of the thirties, and the post-1940 era have all been climactic periods in the history of prophetism and Negro separatist churches. Third, these movements are not confined within colonial boundaries but spread across them. Fourth, these movements are mainly a kind of religious reaction to Christianity, but they are very much more than that alone. "They have the character of a total reaction to a situation which has provoked deep social changes and imposed the notion of inferiority": the Western impact on African societies. "They show how the attempts at social reconstruction and the reactions to the colonial situations are interconnected."

Three examples of prophetism and Negro churches were discussed. The first, Kimbangism, is named after its prophet-founder, Simon Kimbangou, who created it in the Belgian Congo about 1921. Ritual and beliefs reflect Christian teachings. (Kimbangou received knowledge of Christianity from a Prostestant mission.) The founder is sent by God and is His son; baptism, confession, and hymns are part of the ritual. "The protestation and subversion motives which appear in the Bible are utilized in these songs." "The hymns . . . are a sort of 'resistance' literature with Christian pretexts. The administrative authorities have frequently pointed out, in special reports, that the hymns refer to the struggle against white domination and that 'it is always a question of hardships, of misery endured, and of struggles against the enemy.' " The dogma of Kimbangism "respects the most permanent elements of the traditional order: polygamy and ancestor cults. The ancestors are considered capable of intevening to favor the development of an ideal society." The teaching opposes obedience to the colonist, European missionaries, and local administration; all these being closely associated in the Congo. The movement is one of counter-racism in answer to the racism developed by the colonists.

Kimbangism is important but is not a widespread belief affecting great numbers of the Ba-Kongo tribal group. There are other movements, of which Matowanism is an example. It has a distinctly different origin and development.

André Matowa founded his movement in French territory about 1927. It was organized first in France and in the Congo as the *Association Amicale des Originaires de C' A. E. F.* In its origin it was exclusively political and action-oriented. The Association fought against ideas of native inferiority, economic exploitation, and discriminatory codes. It fought for the right to vote. The French colonial administration failed in its attempt to end the movement, but its repressive effort contributed to an important change in the character of Matowanism: it became a movement of total racial opposition. The most fundamental change of all was effected by the death of Matowa, while he was imprisoned. His followers were convinced of his immortality and made of him a semihuman, semi-divine person, "Jesus-Matowa," whose return they expect. In elections, they do not vote for the candidates presented but vote for him. The movement has become institutionalized with a priestly hierarchy, temples, and religious literature.

Among the Ba-Kongo peoples there is a third movement which was discussed at the conference: Kakism. Its founder, a former officer of the Salvation Army, demonstrated unusual organizational ability. The movement has a pronounced racial character. It is a Negro church with a precise ritual of public confession, prayers, and singing meetings. In its form and obligations it attempts to organize and constitute an African society, stressing the fragmentation of tribal groups and ways under the impact of the contemporary world. The movement is unitary in that it is spreading its influence through Angola, and Belgian and French Congo. "In a way of its own, it is trying to make the limits of the new church coincide with a united Congo." In large part, Kakism is an expression of a desire for religious and political autonomy and greater access to material goods. Its racist character is clear and important.

Several observations were made on Kimbangism, Matowanism, and Kakism. Their followers remain aloof from the more ordinary political and trade-union movements. Their leaders are deeply marked by Western influences; they represent an attempt to unite conflicting beliefs and ways in the creation and development of a new society in which racism plays a strong part. These movements do not separate religion from politics but represent a union of the two. They have made a basic contribution to the dawning African "national" consciousness.

Finally, all three movements "aim at a reconstruction of Congo society. They substitute for the ancient and rival cults a unitarian religion. They created a new code of moral prescriptions better adapted to the modern Congo society. They attempt to go beyond the narrow limits of the tribal and clan groups to favor the birth of a society built on a wider basis." "The separatist church, then, is trying to give the African a new aim, a new orientation to make his life meaningful. . . . The separatist churches are important as a new dynamic force in African society. They give new values to the society and many of them try to express Christianity in the African idiom. For instance, in a church like the Shembe Church, there are new sex mores . . . [and] a new set of relationships based on the old Zulu forms or old tribal forms of behavior. In the Shembe Church the relationships are now ritualized . . . . [In a] Shembe prayer book you find two or three pages of injunctions to the father, 'Teach your son to respect the mother,' 'respect your father and respect your mother.' They are trying to instill the values of society that . . . were taken away by the impact of outside influences. They teach also new values like the dignity of labor. In these churches, and particularly the Shembe Church, they have ritualized work. Every morning they pray, and as soon as the prayer is over they get to their homes and out to work in the fields."

One of the prevalent beliefs drawn from Christianity, Islam, and Buddhism and incorporated into separatist churches concerns the "Black Christ." According to them, Christ was sent to the white people, Mohammed to the Arabs, and Buddha to the Eastern peoples. The time is approaching when a Black Savior will lead his own chosen people.

The dynamism of these prophetic Negro church movements reflects the nature of the relationship between Negroes and whites. They are most vigorous in areas where colonialism is experienced most.

Role of Christian Missions. In considering these examples of prophetism and separatist churches it became obvious that missionaries had played an important, if unwitting, part in their creation. In the light of the very extensive and old mission movement and the appearance of separatist churches, several conference members asked questions concerning the general effect of Christian mis-

sions on Africans since the length of their endeavor must have
made an impact upon African thinking and action. Christian missions were considered to be part of the "civilizing" effort of white,
European man. Why has the effort failed in so many cases? Why
have the new African churches departed so markedly from the
Christian pattern? Why is it that African church movements contain such a large element of racism? Westerners find these questions difficult to answer. We would prefer to think that the Christian church and teachings would be the last of Western institutions
and ideas to spawn racism.

According to an African member, "missions and missionaries have
been the creators of much tension" throughout Central and South
Africa. Tensions have developed between white groups themselves,
many of which represented different sects and practices. Tension
was created, for example, within the white communities by reports
of British missions pertaining to relations between South African
Dutch and Africans. While these tensions were occasionally important, the more significant tensions produced by missions were
between the whites and the Africans.

These tensions were and are today of two kinds. First, there is
the unrest and disaffection which inevitably follows the propagation
of Christian principles and, in mission schools, the teaching of a
liberal education in a colonial area. The African gains ideas of
equality, political freedom, and democracy; he acquires a new
conception of himself, becomes more conscious of his status, and
seeks to regain his dignity. Second, the educated African, who has
usually received some mission schooling, is also the prime target
"of the concentrated prejudice of the white men." According to
those whites, the educated African is, by definition, trying to be a
"black Englishman," "getting above himself"; other well-known
epithets are applied . (In Africa one witnesses again the paradox
that Western imperialism and Western political ideology and
humanism are responsible in good part, first, for the successful subjection of peoples and, then, for the emergence of individuals and

movements which take ideas from the West to challenge the West.)
Many of the leaders of the prophetic and separatist church movements in Africa broke from those white churches and the "discipline"
in which their inferior status was evident. The continued reluctance
of some missions to place nonwhites in positions of responsibility
was remarked upon by a conference member who said that while it
has come to be the declared policy of the major mission boards to
accept qualified candidates for foreign missions there are as yet only
approximately 200 nonwhite out of some 19,000 American missionaries. The "divine discontent" (of whites) to which General
Smuts referred is now found increasingly among the blacks.

Missions have played an important and a positive role in the
education of contemporary African leaders. For all their failings,
they have been the most significant bearers of Western learning. If
they have discriminated between black and white, they have also
made a number of Africans aware of the Western ideas of human
equality and political freedom. This cannot be denied. An African
member reported mission practices and beliefs, however, had also
had a disintegrating effect on African societies.

Those features of African culture not found in the Western world
were frequently condemned and destroyed. "African dress, for instance, was discarded because it was 'unchristian.' African music
and dance were evil and they were to be discarded. African marriage
customs were evil and unchristian. Native beer was condemned
although the missionary, of course, kept his wine and brandy. African customs such as *lobolo* were condemned as 'buying brides,' although the white men didn't change their custom of dowries and of
giving expensive engagement rings, and the Africans thought that
this too represented a 'purchase.' Christian converts were told not
to associate with their kinsmen who were not Christians; they were
not supposed to go to the African weddings, that is, tribal weddings
. . . Christian converts were isolated from their people." The African
conference member quoted Walter Lippmann: "having lost their
faith, they lost the certainty that their lives were significant." Out

of this loss emerged the separatist church movements which are, as we have seen, an attempt on the part of some Africans to regain stability and confidence in themselves. The movements reflect the form and institutions of the Christian churches with which their founders were familiar.

While negritude may have as yet only limited appeal and is restricted to a few intellectuals, the fact appeared to be that ideas of race are important in its expression, as they are in the cruder, less sophisticated prophetic and separatist church movements. It is this common denominator of racial consciousness and pride which serves to quicken the interest of millions of Africans in other areas of the Continent. Once again, unity is expressed in its widest terms by a sense of racial identification based on color. Will this common denominator prove to be the most effective symbol of African frustrations and desires? Several conference members shared this view and remarked that the growing appeal to race in modern Africa poses a great challenge to Africans who seek some other basic motivating force to African nationalism. It poses a problem of infinite magnitude to those whites who, having introduced some Western practices and concepts of social and political freedom into African society, now react to the mounting pressure of negritude by seeking means for continuing to justify their self-professed superiority. The conference was unable to determine the extent to which negritude was prevalent in other areas of Africa. A safe assumption would be that it is probably found in a great many other sections, but less adequately conceived and developed in one area than in another, owing to differences in contact with the West and the policies of colonial powers.

There are two important processes working among Africans: one with a limited appeal—negritude—attracting more "Westernized" African leaders, and the other exemplified by those church movements with far greater mass appeal. These two make up the central racist theme and may prove to be the most powerful organizing forces in contemporary Africa. Insofar as the white response does not have as its objective the steady enlargement of the area of freedom for all, those involved are experiencing a dangerous tightening of tensions over issues which are considered by all participants to be of fundamental importance.

African racism will not, however, be similar in all respects to the Western model. The latter served primarily to justify privilege and control. African racism reflects three pressures: the need to reassert one's 'dignity and pride, which is, therefore, a counter-racism to the whites'; the need to re-enforce African societies and customs to meet the conditions of the modern world; and, finally, the conscious use of blackness as a unifying factor—perhaps the only symbol available at this time. African racism has not yet attracted to itself those conceptions of uniqueness or superiority found in the West; at the moment, it appears to be rather a way of asserting one's equality.

Chapter 7

THE FURTHER STUDY OF RACE

Quotations in this chapter are from the unpublished reports of two Race Relations in World Perspective Conference commissions: the Conference Commission on Industrialization and Urbanization, and the Conference Commission on Democratic Institutions in Multiracial Societies.

A major objective of the conference was the discovery of gaps in our knowledge of race relations. During the sessions a number of questions were raised which many conference members thought merited close study.

In the closing sessions of the conference, some members were dismayed at the reluctance of the majority to consider a "doctrine" for race studies; others were disturbed at the broad hospitality given the term "race." Still others sought to restrict research proposals to certain aspects of race, in the belief that more comprehensive and profitable findings would result. Many of these views were proffered by men of unquestioned competence. However, no limits proved feasible and no "doctrine" possible. While conference discussions were often incomplete, for the remarks were necessarily brief, most conference members regarded the meetings as a series of opportunities to exchange ideas on a host of subjects rather than to arrive at a neat conceptual scheme for the further study of race. The lasting impression of the conference on this observer came from being introduced to new fields of inquiry whose boundaries overrun all disciplines and in which a series of complex, exceedingly important events and movements are taking place. No satisfactory academic tools exist for measuring these phenomena, and our understanding of them is, accordingly, imperfect.)

However, despite these limitations, anyone concerned with human relations in political, economic, or social fields recognizes the special urgency of learning as much as possible in the shortest period of time. No one could have listened to the conference discussions and read the papers on race in Africa without sensing the overwhelming importance of knowing far more than we do today about the ideas and use of race which are disturbing millions of Africans. Similarly, American conference members were reminded frequently of the commanding position of the United States, and questions were asked about the effect American racial experiences and views will have on other peoples. (During the conference a news item from Bermuda reported that segregation policies were being considerd there for the first time because of the importance of American tourists.) Such questions emphasized the continuing need for race studies in the United States as well as in so-called underdeveloped lands.

Three commissions were created to examine more closely issues raised during the conference. The first, already mentioned, was the Commission on Race Relations in World Perspective, which restricted its activity to a report and recommendations for research in the historical background of modern race problems. This commission reflected more the views of the European members in its stress on the need for knowledge of the origins of race settings and the spread and influence of ideas of race. Research suggestions were placed under four headings: "Western Racial Ideas," "Problems of Groups and Individuals in Situations of Racial Inequality," "Ideologies of Revolt," and "New Situations."

Western Racial Ideas

On a number of occasions references were made by conference members to contradictions within Western civilization. These contradictions are represented in the belief in human equality of Christendom and the concept of political freedom and, in contrast, the undeniable expressions of racism and race superiority which have developed in so many areas over which Western man has extended his control. There is a need for a general study of the "idea of white superiority seen as a product of changing ideas in Western civilization and of the expansion of Europe, with particular reference to the groups which carried that expansion—traders, missionaries, administrators, and soldiers." A corollary to such a study would be a closer examination of the racial ideas expressed by these groups in the various imperial systems of the British, French, Dutch, Spanish, and Portuguese. An important element in the general and particular case studies would be evidence of those changing ideas within Europe which modified in time the policies and eventually some of the views and practices of colonials. A third recommendation for study was the image of the black man in modern Western civilization: How has he been conceived in Western literature and history? What general view of the black man has gained widespread acceptance, and in what ways and for what reasons has this image changed? (An interesting study could be made, for example, of the American Negro as he has been portrayed in the ubiquitous comic strip, in the American theatre, and in political cartoons.) How much rewriting of the place of the Negro in American history has occurred in the past quarter-century? How much of this re-evaluation reflects sentimentality, how much an awakened consciousness of the role of racism in our history? What are the stereotypes of today? How much is distortion of what we actually believe to be historical fact to conform in 1955 to what we think should have been the attitudes of our forebears? Can similar national studies be made of other peoples' conceptions of Negroes or other racial groups? It would be instructive to examine changing Communist images of the black man, the Jew, the South American Indian, and the Oriental.

Situations of Racial Inequality

The contribution of the Australian conference member on "Cargo Cults," and reports on Israel and the Negro immigrant in

Britain impressed participants and led to a number of suggestions for
studying natives-in-transition: the persons who lead a "double life,"
adapting "themselves externally to alien ways of thought and life
while retaining their convictions and habits beneath the surface."
Such studies should be made of entire communities as well as of specific individuals. In the case of general community analyses, stress
might be placed on the role of traditional and Western-style institutions, both as inhibitors and as vehicles of change. An example is
the persistent, if ebbing, influence of tribal authority versus the
influence and role of African benevolent societies, social clubs,
political associations, and unions. In studies of a particular native-
in-transition, stress might be placed on his role as a leader in
"modernization." What personal characteristics appear to be essential for one to exercise such leadership? What particular experiences
may be common in the lives of a number of these innovators? At
what point and for what reasons does a native alter his course from
being an imitator of Western ways, seeking acceptance by the
dominant group and security from association with it, to a course
which leads to renewed interest in the past, a renovation and
modification of indigenous institutions and customs, and, finally, to
nationalism?

More questions should be asked concerning the "role of religious
systems in racially mixed societies—as solvents of inequality, as justifying inequality, and as expressing the protest of the dominated
groups." Conference discussions of the African prophetic and separatist church movements and the New Guinea "Cargo Cults" focused attention on the importance of a religious system, both as a
cushion which lessens the shock of alien impact and as a positive
power providing an essential unity greater than the tribe or clan, at
the same time acting as the agent of and legitimizing change itself.

What ideologies of integration develop to justify the mixture of
racially and culturally different groups? Specific reference was made
to the West Indies and the Andean regions of South America. Once
again, the Soviet Union's ideology is relevant and the example of

Hawaii pertinent.⟩ In making such studies, one would have to be careful to determine whether all groups of a mixed society are involved in the development of an ideology justifying racial and cultural mixture. In the cases of the Soviet Union and of Hawaii, observers might find, for example, that the development of the ideology and continuing reference to it occurs largely within one group— the European Russian Communists of the Soviet Union and the historically dominant minority of those of European origin in Hawaii—while the *practice* of racial and cultural intermixing occurs chiefly in other segments of the populations.

The dilemma of Israel was cited during the conference and serves as another important instance of integration. The concept of Jewry, powerful as an ideological expression, became less useful with the establishment of Israel. It is clear that Western Jews had in mind a national home with institutions and customs reflecting their European background. The majority of Israeli are, however, of Oriental Jewry; organized groups and religious leaders have stressed the desirability of an Israel run on strictly Orthodox lines. Israel may be useful as an example of a geographically scattered people, linked strongly by their religion and the vision of Zion, finding in their ideology the ways of integration. With the creation of their state, the ideology becomes inadequate, and integration, if it is to occur, must take place largely on conditions set by either the Western Jews or the Oriental Jews. Israel began with the ideology which sanctioned integration, and is now in a sense, divided; the Soviet peoples were fragmented and have been given an ideology. In Hawaii, a compartmented community accepted the unifying American creed even though today the practice of it varies considerably.

In situations of racial inequality, further consideration must be given to the "place of people of mixed races in conflicts between ruling groups of European origin and indigenous communities emerging into political consciousness." General studies have been made of the Eurasian and of the Anglo-Indians. Commission members suggested that studies of these peoples be continued, but that studies also be made of those situations in which the racially mixed rise to the top. The examples of the mestizo in Mexico and in the Philippines were cited. Much more needs to be known concerning the problem of the Cape colored (the racially mixed group of the Union of South Africa), and of the Creoles of Sierra Leone. While in most cases the racially mixed do not form a large part of the population, they often contain elements of race tragedy insofar as the racially mixed are regarded by the indigenous peoples as not belonging and by the dominant group as not acceptable. The racially mixed may have certain privileges such as reserved occupations, government representation, and legal rights denied the indigenous peoples, as was the case in India. In Southern Asia the racially mixed have identified themselves with the West; with national independence their position became one of great difficulty.

There are other situations in which a group of people finds itself between the ruling and the indigenous communities, yet is not racially a mixture of the two. The overseas Chinese and Indians have formed such middle groups in East Africa, Southern Africa, the West Indies, Southern Asia, and in the Pacific. In the past, their interests have been identified exclusively with neither the indigenous nor the ruling groups. Politically they have been neutral, with economic interests in both. In South Africa their political neutrality has gradually been breaking down as a result of the Union's placing of Indians in an unassimilable category along with Africans. In Southern Asia, governments such as Ceylon, Indonesia, Thailand, and the Philippines have adopted national policies leading to assimilation or deportation. Since many of these problems involve great Asian powers, their resolution will have a continuing effect on inter-Asian relations and, in the case of Kenya and the Union of South Africa, on European-Asian affairs.

Ideologies of Revolt

Research suggestions on ideologies of revolt stemmed from conference discussions on race and nationalist movements, with specific reference to prophetic, separatist church movements in Africa and the Pacific Cargo Cults. While emphasis was placed on the extent to which these movements reflected a spirit of "revolt," it was made clear that they were also movements which preserved some features of indigenous African society and culture and yet utilized ideas and practices of the West. In this sense they could be studied as movements which make revolt less likely, for they serve importantly as emotional outlets for frustrated and confused peoples.

With respect to negritude, a suggestion of several members called for a study of "the way in which a word used to express feelings gradually acquires intellectual content by attracting to itself ideas from other contacts, and itself becomes a factor in the situation."

While the image of the black man was a suggested study in the context of Western racial ideas, the image of the white man is of equal importance. How is the white man conceived "in the modern literature and art of various nonwhite civilizations: West Africa, East Africa, Central and South Africa, a group of Southeast Asian countries (e.g., Indonesia, Thailand, Malaya)?" What changes have occurred in this conception? The conference member from India reported there had not been racial animosity in Indian-British relations, only anti-imperialist expressions. Now that the British have left, he asserted, there are no animosities, only differences on specific political and economic issues. Other conference members thought differently and suspected there had been a degree of racial feelings involved, which may not have disappeared entirely with independence. This is an important point, for the extent to which racial views enter into East-West political issues becomes of basic concern, particularly if a comparative study of Russian-Asian relations indicates a relative absence of this racial factor. Such a study would include discussion of "the ideas and feelings of the elites in Africa and Southeast Asia, with particular reference to the role played by the idea of race."

The assumption that nationalist movements in Africa express

themselves fundamentally in racial terms may be made too readily. Because of this, several members urged "a comparative study of nationalist movements in Africa south of the Sahara insofar as they draw their dynamism and unifying power from racial ideologies." Such a study would have its necessary parallel in an examination of the ideologies of conflicts in French North Africa: studies of "situations in which group relations analogous to those existing in areas of racial conflicts can express themselves in ideologies *other than that of race."*

Not included specifically in this commission report, but referred to frequently during conference sessions, was the variety of tactical uses to which race may be put. Race may be a unifying symbol only, or it may be a positive force in the glorification of one color or one physical or cultural characteristic; it may be also a combination of the latter and distinct animosity toward another color or characteristic. The uses of racism could be examined profitably in studies of nationalist movements before and after their achievement of national freedom. What begins, perhaps, as a racial animosity toward whites is altered when freedom is obtained. Ideas and feelings about race may become transformed and redirected. The modern history of Burma and China would be instructive in this respect. (The British and French communities in Canada might be examined also against the background of achievement of dominion status, including specific political issues such as Canadian involvement in European wars and the important place of French Canadians in the Dominion's national politics.)

The conference showed interest in the way and extent to which racial conflicts are transmitted from one area to another. The commission suggested "a study of the way in which the South African problem has been communicated to other African regions and has become a factor in the evolutionary nationalist movements." Finally, the need was stressed for comparative studies of the religious content and significance of a number of movements generated by the contact of Africans, South American Indians, and Pacific Islanders

with the West. We need to know a great deal more of their development and leadership, of the spiritual and ideological content of these
movements, and of the ritual employed.

New Situations

Studies of race relationships in nationalist movements are
important, but since World War II a number of peoples have gained
their political freedom, and their race relationships must be re-ex-
amined under new conditions. Case studies were recommended of
new situations in which the problems of adjustment of whites and
nonwhites must take place: "Senior British officials in Nigeria,
American advisers in the Philippines, Dutch businessmen in Indonesia, United Nations experts in underdeveloped areas, French party
politicians in West Africa, Asian and African nationalist politicians
in power, and Asian and African leaders in the United Nations and
in Commonwealth conferences." Case studies are necessary of the
administrative policies adopted by newly formed or independent nations toward their own minority groups not necessarily white. The
policies of the government of Israel, the Union of Burma, the Philippines, India, Ceylon, and Indonesia would be pertinent.

A continuing study should also be made of the ideologies of
those "national groups which are acquiring new power and influence
in the world: with particular reference to the residue of racial ideas
which remain in those ideologies, and to the changes which power
and influence are bringing about in their own political philosophies
and institutions."

New tensions are appearing within world-society on a basis other than
that of racial difference, and new patterns of power and influence are emerging. Some of the European nations still retain an invisible presence by virtue
of their economic strength and technical skill, even in countries from which
they have formally withdrawn; and the Commonwealth exerts great influence
even though direct British power is less than it was. But other national
groups, too, are rising to influence. The economic strength of the United
States gives her a vast influence over a great part of the Western world;
in and beyond the world of the Indian Ocean there is felt an Indian influence

of which the nature and extent are still unclear; there is a potential Chinese supremacy in East and Southeast Asia; and the Russian people dominate Soviet Eurasia. In regard to each of these nations, a student of race relations may ask certain important questions. What ideas will each elaborate in order to explain and justify its influence and the actions it undertakes? Within those ideas, what residue will remain from the racial theories which have haunted the history of the last century?

There is time lag, not only when power declines, but when it grows. Some peoples find themselves in a position of leadership almost before they are aware of it; and some have nothing in their accepted political philosophies which prepares them for their position of world influence. Marxist universalism did not foresee the growth of Russian and Chinese Communist empires; Indians influenced by the ideas of Gandhi are now facing the responsibilities of a new position in the world; the ideas and attitudes of the American people have not yet adapted themselves to the new role of the United States in world affairs. Americans are in effect the residual legatees of European world power; and they have not yet quite emerged from the racial tension which has been one of the central themes of their history. How far will these factors influence the changes that are likely to come in American ways of thought and life, now that the ideas of democracy are confronted by the fact of power?

Related to such a continuing study would be consideration of the "linguistic, religious, and racial factors in the formation of newly independent national communities in Asia and Africa, and in the mergent conflicts between these communities: e.g., the new states of Southeast Asia."

The commission suggested an examination of the attitude of world Communism toward racial problems and the factors on which those attitudes are based. This analysis might concentrate on Communist attitudes toward non-Communist world race problems and be focused on the multiracial states.

Industrialization and Urbanization and Race Situations

A second conference commission concerned itself with suggestions for research and analysis in the world-wide process of industrialization and urbanization. These suggestions gain an added significance when problems of race relations are considered in the context of economic development schemes. "Industrialization and urbanization are plainly of major importance in the study of race relations. Through these historical processes, peoples of diverse origin have come into contact and have developed ways of working and living alongside one another." While the great "majority of the world's population neither work in factories nor live in towns," as these processes spread "so will increasing numbers of people be brought into new situations of conflict, stress, and adjustment. The social forces generated by these processes undermine traditional loyalties, reshape old ways of thinking and acting, and develop new institutions and relations, many of which may be phrased in terms of racial allegiance." The commission stressed its emphasis on the close relationship between urbanization *and* industrialization, and not on one to the exclusion of the other.

The commission report began by suggesting that research problems be separated and grouped on the basis of whether a problem has primarily an economic or social focus. Studies of the industrialization process would be included in the former and of urbanization in the latter. Within the two areas of inquiry further subdivisions are necessary; there should be, for example, distinctions "based on successive phases of development, from a pre-industrial base-line through a traditional phase to mature industrialism."

Race relations become an issue when capital, skills, and technology are introduced into one area from another. With this introduction the first phase begins. We should know the conditions at the time of importation, much more about the changes that take place following it. We should know more of the phase wherein the area becomes developed, becomes part of the world market, and in time perhaps becomes itself an exporter of capital, skills, and technology.

With respect to these phases we need to ask:

What features of the social organization and culture of the importing area before industrialization impede industrial development, and which features facilitate it? What institutions in the pre-industrial society can be manipulated by outsiders, and what notions and situations, as for example, attitudes to work and opportunities for technological innovation, influence the industrialization process? What kinds of skills are present, to what extent are persons sentimentally involved in technical processes, what is the significance of an attachment to land, what motives and rewards are offered for what kinds of activity? [The African mining companies and Southeast Asian plantation systems would be useful topics in exploring these questions.]

What kinds of people are involved, and how are they differentiated? In particular, how does the type of entrepreneurship affect the form and content of racial and ethnic relationships [as in Malaya or Hawaii]? For instance, how do these relationships vary as between the plantation and the mining corporation, the small settler and large-scale corporate agriculture, or as between the commercial company and the secondary industry? What relationship prevails between the entrepreneur and the government of the area; and how is this related to successive stages of industrial development?

What kinds of managerial, technical, and labour forces are needed, and whence do they come? What are the sources of capital and its ownership, and what measure of control is exercised over its use? How is the labour force recruited and controlled? How does it become differentiated along racial lines, and how do these groups fade away or [how are they] redefined? How do imported skills, and even imported personnel become naturalized? What differences may exist in this respect between primary and secondary economic enterprises, and between urban and rural locations?

Parts of Soviet Central Asia and the Far East could be considered in the light of the following:

How is the labour force created and maintained? What are the effects of coercion, including slavery and forced labour, and when are these institutions considered essential for industrial development? What part do political and legal devices play in structuring the labour force? How do motivations and incentives become related to the new pattern of economic activity and the new social order that emerges? How does a more-or-less fluid labour market get established? When and how does the entrepreneur try to create or rely upon a labour market? When and why do people put themselves into the labour market or withdraw themselves from it? What are the social processes of continued labour migration?

What are the emergent institutions that accompany the industrialization process, both during the transitional and the mature phases, related to education, the law, family and kinship organization, religion, etc.? How do economic wants based on the pre-industrial system give way to those based on the new, both for the producer and the consumer?"

In many Asian areas it is important to have an understanding of the circumstances in which new vested interests develop and when "persons seek to maintain an interest in both the new and the old systems" also:

What kinds of leadership emerge, what forms of organization, and how are these related to notions of race? What is the specific role of strawbosses and other intercalary men who articulate separate fields of organization and ideas?

How do differential rates of fertility and survival affect relations between racially defined groups [as in Australia, New Zealand, Hawaii, the United States, and Africa], and how do differences of numbers, either real or imagined, influence these relations? In particular, how do differences between urban and rural rates of survival lead to social and spatial movement, and how is this related to successive phases of the industrialization process?

When do towns offer an escape from racial classification, or how can they contribute to its continuation through the existences of ghettos? How do urban and rural racial classifications and stereotypes differ from one another and how is this related to changing social conditions? What kinds of urban aggregations grow up on the different kinds of industrial frontiers? What contribution do the cities make to the diversification of views and actions in racially defined situations?

In all these various aspects of the process, a distinction would be drawn between what actually takes place and the perception of what is taking place present in the minds of the actors concerned. In particular, in what ways do those involved in these shifting situations develop, maintain, modify, and abandon perceptions of one another in terms of race?

Democratic Institutions in Multiracial Societies

A third and smaller conference commission on democratic political institutions in a multiracial society issued its report. It defined "democracy" as government by the people, where the sovereign power resides in them as a whole and is expressed either directly or indirectly by elected representatives, and where the people have equal rights without arbitrary or hereditary differences of rank or privilege. The commission report noted that these conditions have been met usually in relatively homogeneous societies. Obviously, serious problems arise when an effort is made to institute appropriate political institutions in multiracial societies where there may be no unity based on a common cultural tradition, common historical experiences, or even an appreciation of a national entity. Where

these conditions do not exist some modification of the Western
institutional form is necessary.

An important modification comes with the need to represent
minority groups (cultural, religious, and racial) and regional
interests. A further problem stems from illiteracy and widespread
inexperience in democratic procedures.

The following suggestions were forwarded by the commission
as meriting consideration. First, a comparative study of attempts
in multiracial societies to foster a "positive, functional unity,"
against a background of revolutionary pre-independence nationalist
ideologies carried over and into the period of national freedom with
new responsibilities. What role does race play in this effort? Second,
attention should be given to the effort of multiracial states to develop
a sound economy drawing upon all elements in the population.
What role does race play in foreign economic relationships? Third,
a comparative study of the forms of political institutions adopted
in multiracial countries which have accepted Western democratic
principles. A study of the assimilation of all racial groups in Hawaii
into its government without reserved seats and powers could be
compared with a similar study of Fiji, Burma, and India.

International Society for the Scientific Study of Race Relations

A great number of these questions put forward by conference members called for comparative study of race relations in
various parts of the world. By studying the events in one area
insight might be gained into developments of another. As the conference proceeded it became clear to the majority that no international organization existed which could concentrate on studies of
race relations. An important result of the conference was, therefore,
the decision to found such a body, which would take up many of
the conference themes and encourage the further study of race—
the International Society for the Scientific Study of Race Relations.
There were several who hoped an "action" organization would

result, but most appeared to be concerned chiefly with the encouragement of further research into many of the contemporary problems discussed—confident that if the studies were sufficiently precise and objective they would be of important aid to other scholars, administrators, observers, and politicians. This latter view was held by the great majority and it prevailed in the new Society. (E. Franklin Frazier, Chairman of the Sociology Department of Howard University, was elected Chairman; Quintin A. Whyte, Director of the South African Institute of Race Relations, Vice-chairman; and William O. Brown, Director of the African Research and Studies Program, Boston University, Secretary-Treasurer.)

The Society is nongovernmental and independent. It has several important purposes. A primary function is to act as an international clearing house for information on research projects. Through the Society, scholars and others interested in race relations will be able to learn of individuals and organizations active in this field. The conference introduced the members to race situations and different analyses of race problems in many parts of the world. The Society will continue that association, and will facilitate the greater flow of information necessary to continue studies of race in world perspective

In time, the Society hopes to be able to encourage the creation of research institutes on problems of race relations in those areas where the facilities for such studies do not exist, or to assist the efforts of those who have initiated studies but could use further help. A majority of the conference members thought the resources of the Society might be employed more effectively in efforts to keep students of race relations in touch with each other and to encourage the work of local research groups.

In line with the broad definition of "race" used by most conference members, the Society welcomes all disciplines which can make a contribution to our knowledge of race. Conference discussions revealed common denominators in many race situations scattered around the world. With this background, the international char-

acter of the Society will permit it to encourage comparative studies
which will help in the formulation of general propositions concerning race relations. From such propositions we should gain greater
understanding of the complex phenomena of race in our contemporary world. It is possible that this objective of the Society will be
its most useful contribution to the further study of race situations.

Race in World Perspective

In the preceding pages those aspects of race which appeared
to be of most interest to the majority of conference members have
been traced. No conference session was considered to have exhausted
a topic, and it is impossible to speak of any conclusions reached.
Conference members gained most value from reports of race situations when the discussion leader gave insight into the complex issues
involved, enabling other members to compare and contrast factors
present in one area with those in another. Relatively little attention was paid to conceptual schemes or theoretical critiques as such;
conference members were more concerned with discovering the common factors in race situations in the New World, Asia, Africa, and
the Pacific.

The common denominator of all race situations discussed was
their *dynamic* character. Race situations reflect the major political,
economic, and social changes of our time. Whether reference is
made to the situation of natives of New Guinea or the African
mechanic of the Congo, the American Negro teacher or the Indian
peasant of Peru, each of these situations has felt the impact of
change and is still evolving.

The changes in the foci of great international political and
economic power—especially the decline of Western empires—have
had an important effect in many areas of Africa and Asia. A major
result has been the achievement of political freedom for millions.
Many of these have been faced with acute minority problems of
their own and have been forced to recognize them in government
policy and laws. Changes in Western racial attitudes have also

played an important part in evolving race situations. The increasing involvement of all areas of the world in international trade has itself enlarged the interests of many groups of people. Improved communications and greater opportunities for travel have enlarged the horizons of many hitherto isolated peoples and brought them into more frequent contact with other groups considered to be racially different. These changes have had an undeniable influence on race situations, sometimes lessening tension and sometimes increasing it.

The critical importance of many of these changes was evident at the beginning of the conference, when the broadest hospitality was given definitions of "race." From the outset, conference members concerned themselves with situations in which differences of race, actual or supposed, played a part in human relationships. The conference did not attempt only to examine *race* as defined by the natural scientists, but was interested in the extent of the influence of ideas *about* race and the use of race as a factor in contemporary movements.

In many cases, ideology was considered to be as important in race situations as economic or political forces. It was obvious, for example, that nationalism in Africa, the Pacific, and Southeast Asia contains an element of "race" which cannot be ignored any more than economic or political interests, expressed through race attitudes, can be discounted. The emerging, indigenous leadership of Africa, of parts of Asia, of the Near East, among New Guinea natives, and among Australian aborigines owes some of its vitality to Western ideas and institutions. If some of those ideas have inspired a number to achieve political freedom, others have engendered a consciousness of race; and it is the compound of race and nationalism which poses special problems in East-West relationships.

The study of situations in which a race factor exists requires a comprehensive understanding of the whole society. No concentration on one aspect to the exclusion of others will suffice; all aspects of the society must be considered. Furthermore, owing to the dynamic character of race situations, no static concept or "doctrine" of race is yet possible. We are still engaged in the dual task of gathering information and searching for general propositions which will give greater meaning to the data. In this respect the greatest value of the conference lay in the examination of race situations from a world perspective.

Three final impressions of the conference impart a special sense of urgency to the further study of race:

First, racism may be losing its vitality in most of the Western world. It remains important, however, in the ideas and responses of millions of people who experienced it at the hands of Western man. It may find a new vitality in the nationalist movements now developing in Africa. If this proves to be true, it will be of consequence to all peoples—a tragedy of the first magnitude.

Second, while racism in its most outspoken form may be disappearing from some areas, it may actually remain a significant but subtle force expressed in different ways. A glorification of being Asian or African or Western may prove to be little different in fact from pride in being brown or black or white. A people's pride in its cultural past or technological and economic achievements, or stress on any uniqueness, may be, in part at least, only a more sophisticated expression of a deep-seated belief in innate superiority.

Third, while study of the racial attitudes of Western man is necessary, attention should also be directed to studies of race in the historic and contemporary relationships between Asian peoples. Our current emphasis on race as a phenomenon of the Western world or as a factor in the response of indigenous peoples to the ideas and actions of Western man may have caused us to overlook similar phenomena in the ideas and actions of Asians, particularly of the Chinese, Japanese, and Indian peoples.